WITH GOD

I ALWAYS HAVE HOPE

A 90-DAY DEVOTIONAL

Chosen

a division of Baker Publishing Group
Minneapolis, Minnesota

© 2022 by Baker Publishing Group

Published by Chosen Books
11400 Hampshire Avenue South
Minneapolis, Minnesota 55438
www.chosenbooks.com

Chosen Books is a division of
Baker Publishing Group, Grand Rapids, Michigan

Printed in the United States of America

ISBN 978-0-8007-6242-1 (trade paper)
ISBN 978-1-4934-3584-5 (ebook)

Library of Congress Control Number: 2021043598

Written by Austin Coleman, Maurice Gavin, Nikki Harris, Hope Johnson and Samantha Vocarte

Cover design by Studio Gearbox

22   23   24   25   26   27   28   7   6   5   4   3   2   1

CONTENTS

Introduction   7

1. God's Good Plans   10
2. The Triumph of Love   12
3. God with Us   14
4. Small, Yet Mighty   16
5. A Laugh Redeemed   18
6. Hope in Grief   20
7. God's Persistent Voice   22
8. The Peace Christ Gives   24
9. Song of Hope   26
10. The God Who Never Lies   28
11. Double Favor   30
12. Hope for Eternal Life   32
13. Hope in God, Not Riches   34
14. Surprised by Hope   36
15. Facing Fiery Trials   38
16. God Loves to Forgive   40
17. Overcoming Unbelief   42
18. Equipped for Your Calling   44
19. Hope in God's Covenant   46
20. The God Who Hears   48

21. God's Plan for Me 50

22. Hope for Spiritual Awakening 52

23. Release and Trust 54

24. Jesus' Perfect Empathy 56

25. Hope in the Glory of God 58

26. Hope in God's Counsel 60

27. Defeating Every Enemy 62

28. God's Perfect Timing 64

29. Supernatural Confidence 66

30. Hope for Understanding 68

31. God's Motives Are Good 70

32. Hope in Jesus' Second Coming 72

33. Words of Life 74

34. A Door of Hope 76

35. Seeing through Spiritual Eyes 78

36. King Jesus, Our Hope 80

37. God's Perfect Promises 82

38. Every Prophecy Fulfilled 84

39. A Well-Watered Tree 86

40. Stepping into Miracles 88

41. Hope for Justice 90

42. Salvation for My Household 92

43. A Second Chance 94

44. Weapons of Hope 96

45. God Sees You 98

46. Hope against All Hope 100

47. Hope for Discernment 102

48. Judgment Removed 104

49. The Friendship of the Holy Spirit 106

50. Hope for a Righteous Ruler 108

51. God's Help in Trouble   110

52. Made for Friendship   112

53. Hope That Acts   114

54. Peace with God   116

55. Deferred Hopes   118

56. God Multiplies Comfort   120

57. Abounding Hope   122

58. Fully Restored   124

59. Hope for a Family Reunion   126

60. Unfailing Mercy   128

61. Scared, Yet Surrendered   130

62. Impossible Provision   132

63. Fresh Life   134

64. Hope in the Promise Keeper   136

65. A Way in the Wilderness   138

66. A Different Spirit   140

67. Hope for Immortality   142

68. God's Merciful Heart   144

69. Relentless Hope   146

70. God Proves Himself   148

71. Hope amid Persecution   150

72. God Goes before Me   152

73. Reconciliation with God   154

74. A Righteous Legacy   156

75. Unashamed Hope   158

76. Hope Anchors Us   160

77. Fear No Man   162

78. Hope in the Living God   164

79. Hope That Doesn't Disappoint   166

80. Hope for New Life   168

81. God Rescues   170

82. Hope for the Unseen   172

83. Remember God's Faithfulness   174

84. Hope Brings Endurance   176

85. Hope in God's Power   178

86. Resurrected Life   180

87. God Protects Me   182

88. The God Who Remembers   184

89. Hope for a Brighter Future   186

90. God Is with Me   188

Special Invitation   191

INTRODUCTION

Whatever you are facing, with God, you always have hope!

God's Word offers you the beautiful gift of hope, empowering you to experience His joy and peace, to face your fears with boldness and to walk confidently into your purpose. The hope you have in Jesus Christ renews your strength (Isaiah 40:31), anchors your soul (Hebrews 6:19) and helps you to live in light of eternity (2 Corinthians 4:18).

This devotional is designed to illuminate the hope you have with God in every circumstance you face—from fighting fear to navigating grief, from waiting on God's promises to hearing God's voice. As you read, you will be reminded of the hope you have in Christ, encouraged to embrace this hope and challenged to act on it. You may want to keep a journal to record your journey of hope.

Each day's reading is two short pages that contain the following:

- A powerful, hope-filled Scripture. Read it purposefully and prayerfully. The Word of God is able to encourage and strengthen.

- An inspirational meditation you can read in under two minutes.
- A personalized reflective question and a prayer to help you talk to God about what you have read.
- An affirmative declaration to repeat throughout your day, which will help lock in a hopeful truth.
- A practical action that will inspire hope and gratitude, encouraging you to step out in faith with the help of the Holy Spirit.

May the words in this book strengthen your faith, open your eyes to God's love and faithfulness and empower you to live your life in light of the truth that with God, you always have hope.

WITH GOD

I ALWAYS HAVE HOPE

1 God's Good Plans

"For I know the plans that I have for you," declares the Lord, "plans for prosperity and not for disaster, to give you a future and a hope."

Jeremiah 29:11 NASB

What does a hopeful future mean to you? If you were to write a short story about your ideal life, drafting it to be full of purpose, prosperity and joy, what would be in that story?

Sometimes God's plans for our lives do not feel good in the moment. Sometimes it feels like our stories have been hijacked and we are leaning more toward disaster than prosperity. This verse from Jeremiah is frequently quoted to encourage believers that God has hopeful plans for our lives. But we often miss the context of the passage. God was speaking to His people as they were in captivity.

The true hope of this passage is that the promises of God are solid in spite of hardships. A difficult present does not indicate a hopeless future. With God, our difficult present is primed to be transformed into the rich future He has orchestrated for us.

God knows exactly where your story is going because He wrote it. Every detail is secured and fashioned with you in mind. Even in the midst of difficulties, you can rest knowing His plans for you are still good and still in motion.

▶ **REFLECT**

What do I feel when I hear God has plans to give me a good future?

▶ **PRAY**

Father, I believe You when You say that You have counted every one of my days. I have hope for my future because You have already gone before me. You have planned my life with care and purpose. Help me to rest in security and trust that Your plans for me are good.

▶ **DECLARE**

God's plans for me are full of hope.

▶ **ACT**

Share with someone a dream for the future that God has planted in your heart.

2 | The Triumph of Love

> So now I live with the confidence that there is nothing in the universe with the power to separate us from God's love. I'm convinced that his love will triumph over death, life's troubles, fallen angels, or dark rulers in the heavens. There is nothing in our present or future circumstances that can weaken his love.
>
> Romans 8:38 TPT

Have you ever been in a relationship in which you had to work in order to feel valued or loved? Jesus' love is far better. Whereas human love is often conditional, His love is unconditional.

People often put conditions on relationships. If I do "this," then they will like me. If I do "that," then they will show me affection. If I don't do certain things, they may not want to relate with me at all. Living in light of these conditions can cause you to go through life with an unhealthy view of love. Rather than viewing love as a gift, you may see love as something you must earn. You may begin to feel that you can never "do" enough to be loved.

The Bible says that the love of Jesus is unconditional. He did not love us because of anything we did; in fact, "while we were still sinners, Christ died for us" (Romans 5:8 NIV). His love is so powerful that nothing you ever "do" or "do not do" can separate you from that love.

You do not have to strive for His love and acceptance; rather, you can rest in the hope of His unconditional love.

▶ REFLECT

When have I most clearly felt Jesus' love?

▶ PRAY

Jesus, I am amazed that You love me completely and unconditionally. There is nothing anyone or anything can do to separate me from Your love. May I not strive for Your love and acceptance, for I already have it. Help me to rest in this truth, no matter how I may feel.

▶ DECLARE

Jesus loves me unconditionally.

▶ ACT

Go to a mirror and repeat the declaration above: "Jesus loves me unconditionally."

3   God with Us

"Behold, the virgin shall be with child, and bear a Son, and they shall call His name Immanuel," which is translated, "God with us."

Matthew 1:23 NKJV

For those who have grown up in a religious setting, this Scripture is all too familiar, as it is read during the holiday season when children anticipate Santa's present-laden arrival.

In our hurry to get to the manger scene and the arrival of the wise men, we inadvertently race past the miraculous nature of the above statement.

God chose to be with us in human form.

To accomplish this, the seed that would be implanted within the virgin Mary would have to come from a supernatural source, without the aid of natural human interaction. A virgin with child . . . amazing! And the child is the direct offspring of the God of Israel's covenant and the Creator of every star, including the star of Bethlehem . . . breathtaking.

God didn't stop there. He then made His Son a living sacrifice for all so that He could be with us throughout eternity as a multinational, divine family.

If God accomplished all this over two thousand years ago without any of our assistance, we can have hope in His ability to solve whatever problem that is top-of-mind right now.

God is with you today in the Person of His Holy Spirit.

▶ REFLECT

What would change in my life if I knew for certain that God was with me?

▶ PRAY

Father, help me discern Your presence daily so I can grow in my awareness of Your being with me. You have chosen to interact with me as a loving Father who sent His Son to save me when I was not seeking salvation. You have chosen to be with me and place value upon me far beyond what I deserve. Help me to see these truths from Your perspective in my daily life.

▶ DECLARE

God is present in my life.

▶ ACT

Set an hourly timer on your watch or phone, and every time you hear the chime, remind yourself that God is with you.

4   Small, Yet Mighty

> The LORD said to Gideon, "The people with you are too many for me to give the Midianites into their hand, lest Israel boast over me, saying, 'My own hand has saved me.'"
>
> Judges 7:2 ESV

Have you ever encountered a situation in which you felt small and inadequate? God wants you to know that you can be strong and powerful in Him regardless of how small you feel.

There will be times in each of our lives when we will experience things, people and situations that incite feelings of insufficiency. Gideon, too, likely felt insufficient to defeat the Midianites, especially when God whittled his army down to only three hundred men. God reduced Gideon's army to display His glory; in a mighty show of strength, God delivered the Midianites into Gideon's hand.

God loves to see us rise to our destiny when the odds are stacked against us. Just as He did with Gideon, often God will allow situations that make us seem small and insignificant only to show us His power and our need to rely on Him. If you are facing a situation in which you feel inadequate, know that God will help you if you rely on Him and do not yield to your own understanding and resolve.

Your weakness submitted to God could be the springboard for the miraculous to occur in your life. Your situation is designed for your good and for God's glory.

▶ REFLECT

How can I shift my focus from my insufficiency to God's power?

▶ PRAY

Father God, help me to hope in Your strength and be courageous in the difficult situations that try to frighten and overwhelm me. Help me to remember that I can do all things through Christ. Help me to remember that because You live inside of me, I have more strength than any opposing force in the world.

▶ DECLARE

I am strong and courageous in Christ.

▶ ACT

Look to the Holy Spirit to guide you in a situation where you need to be strong and courageous, remembering that God is your strength.

5   A Laugh Redeemed

> Sarah said, "God has brought me laughter, and everyone who hears about this will laugh with me." And she added, "Who would have said to Abraham that Sarah would nurse children? Yet I have borne him a son in his old age."
>
> Genesis 21:6–7 NIV

When God has not answered our prayers as we had imagined, it can be hard to maintain joyful expectancy. To avoid disappointment, we may have become cynical, but God invites us to embrace a hope that will *never* disappoint.

When, year after year, Sarah didn't conceive the son God had promised, she donned the armor of cynicism. Sarah was ninety years old when a messenger of the Lord reminded Abraham of the promise, and she laughed cynically (see Genesis 18:1–15). It was easier to replace hope with distrust than to be disappointed yet again.

But Sarah's lack of faith did not dissuade God from fulfilling His promise; a year later, she gave birth to Isaac, whose name means "laughter." In His redemptive love and faithfulness, God replaced her cynical laugh with a joyful one.

God longs to replace your cynicism with joyful hope. He did not fulfill His promise when or how Sarah expected, but His timing proved perfect. As you remember the story of Sarah, lay down your cynicism and take up hope, confident that God will fulfill His promises to you in a way more glorious and meaningful than you can imagine.

▶ REFLECT

In what area do I need to exchange a cynical laugh for a hopeful one?

▶ PRAY

Father God, like Sarah, I have clothed myself in the armor of cynicism to protect myself from disappointment. Help me to shed this cynicism and replace it with the bright garments of hope in Your promises, which never fail. Redeem my cynical laughter by replacing it with joyful expectation as I wait.

▶ DECLARE

God fills me with joyful hope.

▶ ACT

When you feel tempted to react cynically, respond with hopeful words or joyful actions instead.

Hope in Grief

The Lord is close to all whose hearts are crushed by pain, and he is always ready to restore the repentant one.

Psalm 34:18 TPT

Grief is hard, yet God is with you in your grief.

If you have experienced a loss in your life, you know that the brutality of grief is painstaking, and almost nothing eases its grip. The loss of a loved one leaves a gaping hole that time itself cannot repair.

Grief is treacherous when it is absent of hope, blinding us to the faithfulness, kindness and justice of God. Hope in God and His Word is the only real comfort to which a grieving heart will respond, and at times that is hard to grasp. Pain may crush us, yet God is there to knit together the shattered pieces of our hearts.

A grieving heart submitted to hope worships the Lord for His nearness, although we may not feel it in the moment. When we choose hope in the midst of grief, we embrace the power of the Holy Spirit to mend and restore our hearts. The Holy Spirit is assigned to us to minister grace and healing amid our brokenness, and we can trust that He will comfort us in our grief.

You have hope in grief because you are not alone; God is with you.

► **REFLECT**

In what area of loss or grief do I need the comfort of the Holy Spirit?

► **PRAY**

Father God, You promise to be near the brokenhearted. You promise to be close to those who are crushed by pain. You understand the pain of losing a loved one. Father, thank You for the presence of the Holy Spirit in this time of painful grief. Father, thank You that we have hope and we do not have to grieve alone, because You are here.

► **DECLARE**

The Holy Spirit is my Comforter.

► **ACT**

Call someone whom you know is grieving a loss, then invite him or her to coffee or a meal and share words of comfort.

7   God's Persistent Voice

> The LORD came and stood there, calling as at the other times, "Samuel! Samuel!" Then Samuel said, "Speak, for your servant is listening."
>
> 1 Samuel 3:10 NIV

Have you ever compared hearing God's voice to a game of hide-and-seek, fearing that if you do not search hard enough, you will miss your chance to hear Him? Know this: God is not hiding from you; He is *pursuing* you!

When God first spoke to Samuel, the future prophet did not understand that God was speaking to him. Instead of considering Samuel a lost cause, God persistently called until, the third time He spoke, Samuel finally understood who was speaking.

God was not exasperated or dissuaded by Samuel's lack of understanding. Instead, out of His great love and purpose, God repeated Himself to the young boy for whom He had great plans.

The same is true for you as God's child. He does not roll His eyes when you lack understanding; instead, He cherishes your desire to hear His voice. In a patience born of joy for His beloved child, He will speak to you persistently through His Word, His people and the Holy Spirit.

You can seek His voice with the hope and assurance that God is not a God of confusion, but a God of clarity who longs to fill your ears with truth.

▶ REFLECT

What was the last thing I feel God said to me?

▶ PRAY

Loving Father, I praise You that You do not obscure Your voice, but You pursue me passionately with Your truth. You are not a God of confusion, but a God of clarity! Fill me with an ever-increasing desire to hear You. Make Your voice known to me through Your Word, Your people and the Holy Spirit.

▶ DECLARE

God speaks to me, and I hear His voice.

▶ ACT

As you go throughout your day, stop periodically and listen to what God is saying to you.

8   The Peace Christ Gives

"Peace I leave with you, My peace I give to you; not as the world gives do I give to you. Let not your heart be troubled, neither let it be afraid."

John 14:27 NKJV

When Jesus alerted the disciples to His coming betrayal and crucifixion, He took the common Jewish greeting *shalom* (peace) and transformed it into a never-before-revealed bedrock of the Christian experience.

Jesus personalized and then differentiated *shalom* from its common usage by indicating that the *shalom* He gives is something extraordinary. He revealed to His disciples that He was giving them the gift of peace to prepare and empower them for the difficult and confusing times to come: His crucifixion, His three days in the grave and the persecution they would experience after He ascended to heaven. He gave them His peace as someone might give a friend his cloak to help him weather an impending storm.

Yet Jesus clarified that His peace was not the calm, undisturbed state their world offered—typically only experienced during the period after a military victory. Instead, His peace was able to empower those who received it to steady their hearts in times of uncertainty and coming persecution.

Over two thousand years later, we are still empowered to receive Jesus' *shalom* daily to overcome our uncertainties. His peace is tangible, effectual and beyond human comprehension.

▶ REFLECT

Where could I benefit from experiencing Jesus' peace in my life today?

▶ PRAY

Father God, reveal to me the peace that Jesus gives. May it reside in my heart and never leave. Teach me to bring this peace to others that they, too, might know the peace that surpasses understanding. With my focus on Your peace, my faith will rise, and my fears will recede from view.

▶ DECLARE

I have the peace of Christ.

▶ ACT

Speak words of Jesus' peace to someone you know whose circumstances are causing him or her anxiety.

9 Song of Hope

> Then Moses and the sons of Israel sang this song to the LORD, saying: "I will sing to the LORD, for He is highly exalted; the horse and its rider He has hurled into the sea."
>
> Exodus 15:1 NASB

When no one is home, or when you are in your car alone, do you ever sing so only you and God can hear?

This scene in Exodus is much more dramatic than singing in the car. After four hundred years of slavery and ten plagues striking the land of Egypt, the Israelites walked out of captivity, only to be pursued by Pharoah's army to the Red Sea. In one of the most famous passages in Scripture, God parts the waters, the Israelites walk across on dry land and Pharoah's army is swallowed by the collapsing waves.

In moments like this, speeches and words fall short. When life is overwhelming, circumstances are challenging or we witness miracles, it may be time to lift up a song of praise. Hope rises with a melody, and even if it doesn't sound beautiful to your ears, God loves to hear the praises of His children.

So turn up the music today. Let family and friends hear you. Sing about what He has done in the past to give you hope for today, and know your song is precious to Him.

▶ REFLECT

What songs have brought me hope?

▶ PRAY

Father, when I am overwhelmed and in need of hope, I will sing a song to You, my Maker. When I am full of joy and want to praise You, I will sing to You. When I am frightened and need to hear truth spoken over me, I will sing songs of praise to the Author of my life.

▶ DECLARE

I sing to the Lord for who He is and what He has done.

▶ ACT

Sing out a favorite praise or worship song to the Lord.

10   The God Who Never Lies

> So God has given both his promise and his oath. These two things are unchangeable because it is impossible for God to lie. Therefore, we who have fled to him for refuge can have great confidence as we hold to the hope that lies before us.
>
> Hebrews 6:18 NLT

God *always* tells the truth. In a world filled with broken promises, half-truths, and bald-faced lies, you can embrace unshakable hope because God is always faithful to His Word.

If you have been repeatedly disappointed by the promises of the world or of other people, you may look with suspicion on anything that "seems too good to be true." Your trust may have been broken so many times that unbelief seems the most prudent choice.

God's promises are of such great magnitude that they may also seem too good to be true: He has promised us intimate love, forgiveness of sins and eternal life! But His promises are far different from the worldly promises that have disappointed you. As you read through the Scriptures, you can see promise after promise fulfilled, and when you review your own history of walking with God, you will also see how He was faithful, even when others were not.

As you walk through a world that has taught you to trust no one, know that your Savior is nothing like those who have let you down. His promises are true, His love is steady and you can trust Him.

▶ REFLECT

In what situations have I seen God's Word proven to be true?

▶ PRAY

Father God, the broken promises of the world make it hard for me to trust. May I not allow the world's betrayal to taint my belief in Your promises, but may You lead me to a deeper understanding of Your honesty. You are a beacon of unwavering truth in a world of dark deception, and I entrust myself to You.

▶ DECLARE

Every word of God is true.

▶ ACT

Talk with someone about a promise of God you are struggling to believe and ask him or her to pray for you.

11 Double Favor

And when the king saw Queen Esther standing in the court, she won favor in his sight, and he held out to Esther the golden scepter that was in his hand. Then Esther approached and touched the tip of the scepter.

Esther 5:2 ESV

Sometimes you need both God's favor and the favor of other people to accomplish God's will. But He will never give you an assignment without the favor you need to accomplish it.

Queen Esther was faced with the life-threatening task of approaching King Xerxes to save her people from annihilation. She needed favor with both God and the king. Esther engaged in prayer and fasting, and God favored her faithfulness. God moved in the king's heart, and he listened to Esther although he had the right to kill her. This double favor empowered her to complete the task unharmed.

What task is God entrusting you with that you feel inadequate to complete alone? God-sized tasks require double favor. The special grace, wisdom and knowledge that seem to come out of nowhere are all forms of God's favor. God's favor is always available, but it takes discernment to see it. God will also give you favor with just the right people, putting others in your path who will open doors to what God has called you to do.

God will give you all the favor you need to complete His will. Step forward in faith and get ready to see Him work!

▶ REFLECT

Where do I need God's favor most in my life?

▶ PRAY

Father God, I thank You for Your divine favor. Thank You for granting me favor with men to accomplish Your will. Help me to discern Your favor in every situation in my life. Thank You for giving me what I need to do Your will. Help me also to be a source of favor for others doing Your will.

▶ DECLARE

I have favor with God and others.

▶ ACT

Reach out to one person whose favor has allowed you to accomplish God's will and thank him or her.

Hope for Eternal Life

> For our dying bodies must be transformed into bodies that will
> never die; our mortal bodies must be transformed into immortal
> bodies.
>
> 1 Corinthians 15:53 NLT

Imagine the disciples' shock, terror and disbelief when Jesus first appeared to them after His resurrection as if He had walked through the wall.

Next, imagine the stunned silence of the disciples en route to Emmaus, when He revealed Himself at the table and then disappeared after blessing the meal (see Luke 24:13–35).

Finally, feel the bewilderment His disciples must have felt when they handled Him, a risen, yet physical body still bearing the marks of the Roman spearhead in His side and the railroad spike–sized nail wounds in His wrists and ankles that were still open (see Luke 24:36–43).

This post-resurrection Jesus was supernatural, to say the least. We, too, will trade in our aging bodies for a physical covering that will be impervious to the effects of mortality. When we are clothed with immortality, secure in our eternal right standing with God, our hope in Christ will be fulfilled. Not only will we trade our broken bodies for immortal ones, but when we see Him, we shall be like Him! (See 1 John 3:2.)

This hope is difficult to comprehend through our earthly lens. One day, though, our faith will become sight, and we will fall at Jesus' feet in awe of His glory, power, and goodness.

▶ **REFLECT**

What do I think my transformed body will look like?

▶ **PRAY**

Father in heaven, may I focus on things above and not on earthly things as I live in light of eternity. Open the eyes of my heart to see the coming reality of my resurrection, of being clothed with a heavenly physical frame that will allow me to be even more like Jesus.

▶ **DECLARE**

I will have a new body that will never die.

▶ **ACT**

Listen to the Holy Spirit and do one thing today that has eternal value.

13 Hope in God, Not Riches

> Command those who are rich in this present world not to be arrogant nor to put their hope in wealth, which is so uncertain, but to put their hope in God, who richly provides us with everything for our enjoyment.
>
> 1 Timothy 6:17 NIV

Did you know Jesus spoke more about money than almost any other subject? He knew how tempting it was to view worldly riches as a source of salvation. Although riches may offer temporary security, Jesus promises eternal security.

When we find ourselves anxious about how much money we have in the bank, the status of a 401(k) or how we are going to pay off our loans, Jesus reminds us that riches are fleeting. He implores us not to "store up for [ourselves] treasures on earth, where moths and vermin destroy . . . but [to] store up for [ourselves] treasures in heaven" (Matthew 6:19–20 NIV).

God also promises us that when we seek His Kingdom first, He will give us all that we need. He will not withhold any good thing from us. He will take care of us, and what He gives us will be for our enjoyment. We will only be able to enjoy these things without anxiety, though, if our hearts are set on Him rather than on His gifts.

Do not be arrogant and put your hope in your own riches. Put your hope in God and see how richly He provides for you!

▶ REFLECT

What financial concerns have been stealing my peace?

▶ PRAY

Lord, help me to put aside my trust of worldly riches and put my trust in You. You promised You would give me all things to enjoy if I trust in You and seek Your Kingdom first. I trust You and believe Your promise that You will take care of my needs.

▶ DECLARE

The Lord provides for my needs as I seek Him first.

▶ ACT

Tell someone about a financial concern and ask him or her to keep you accountable in your trust for *God's* provision.

14   Surprised by Hope

> "But we had hoped that he was the one who was going to redeem Israel. And what is more, it is the third day since all this took place."

Luke 24:21 NIV

When your hopes are disappointed, you may feel that God has betrayed your trust. You can be assured, though, that He is writing a story of hope in your life more profound and beautiful than you can imagine.

After Jesus died, some of His followers also felt betrayed by their hope (see Luke 24:13–32). They were so convinced they had misplaced their trust that they didn't recognize Jesus when He approached them. Through blurred human vision, they didn't see that what they had hoped for had actually come to pass. The resurrected Redeemer of Israel had answered their hope with more than they had dared to expect: He had killed death, and their redemption was eternal. Jesus walked alongside them, undeterred by their hopelessness, patiently explaining how Scripture pointed to Him until their hearts burned with the truth.

He does the same with you. When your hopes are disappointed and you question His goodness, He walks alongside you, patiently teaching you the truth.

You can trust that just as He opened the eyes of His despairing followers, He will one day open your eyes to the full glory of His work in your life and the ways He has answered your vulnerable hope.

▶ REFLECT

Where does God want to surprise me with hope, possibly with something I think is dead?

▶ PRAY

Father God, just as You opened the eyes of the men on the road to Emmaus, open my eyes to the reality of Jesus' love, His compassion and the absolute goodness of His character. Heal my heart where I feel I have been betrayed by misplaced hope, and help me lay hold of the truth that my hope in You will never disappoint.

▶ DECLARE

God has joyful surprises prepared for me.

▶ ACT

In some way, take a step of faith today toward an area in which you need hope.

15 Facing Fiery Trials

"But if not, be it known to you, O king, that we will not serve your gods or worship the golden image that you have set up."

Daniel 3:18 ESV

God wants you to hope in Him when you are facing fiery trials.

Fiery trials have the potential to strengthen our faith muscles. When we encounter fiery trials, God wants us to know that He can be trusted in them. The three Hebrew teenagers in Daniel 3 had an unwavering trust in God. Even in the face of the fiery furnace and impending death, they knew that regardless of the circumstances, their hope was in God.

Not many of us are called to be martyrs, but we are expected to maintain our faith, trust and hope in God amid frightening circumstances. We should remind ourselves that the circumstances are not bigger than God.

Trials are fierce, but they cannot destroy us without our consent. We must set ablaze our faith-filled hope and demand our circumstances to respect our faith. We must tell our fear, frustration and trials, "We will not serve you, nor will we bow down to you!" Often during the hardest part of a fiery trial, when we are faithful to stand, we are privileged to see God show up for us in the furnace of affliction.

Do not run from the fire, but embrace it, and God will meet you in the midst of it.

▶ REFLECT

In what fiery trial do I want to stand firm and not bow down, regardless of what I see?

▶ PRAY

Father God, I am grateful that You will never leave me or forsake me. God, nothing is more powerful than You. You are all-powerful and trustworthy. Lord, help me to remember that many are the afflictions of the righteous, but You will deliver me out of them all. God, increase my faith and build my hope in You.

▶ DECLARE

God empowers me to stand strong in every circumstance.

▶ ACT

Write a declaration of hope for a fiery trial you are facing and share it with someone who can stand with you.

16 God Loves to Forgive

> If we confess our sins, he is faithful and just and will forgive us our sins and purify us from all unrighteousness.
>
> 1 John 1:9 NIV

God not only forgives your sins, He *delights* in forgiving them! Have you ever avoided confessing your sins out of shame, afraid that God would respond in frustration and anger that you messed up yet again?

Others may respond to your shortcomings with a lack of grace, and your own heart may condemn you, but God forgives without frustration or hesitation. Scripture says that He "has *lavished* [His love] on us, that we should be called children of God!" (1 John 3:1 NIV, emphasis added). His forgiveness is a joyful overflow of His love for you that not only covers your sins but declares you His beloved child. He treats you not as a stranger, but instead He has adopted you.

When you confess your sins, then you must refuse to listen to the voices of shame and condemnation, for they are not from Him. Instead, imagine Jesus beckoning you to run to His open arms, longing for you to understand the greatness of His love.

Jesus loves you so passionately that He went to the cross with wholehearted willingness, and He longs for you to experience the forgiveness that comes from putting your hope in His unreserved, unconditional love.

▶ REFLECT

In what ways might my view of God be preventing me from confessing my sins boldly, assured of His acceptance?

▶ PRAY

Father God, thank You for forgiving me joyfully and declaring me Your beloved child. When my heart condemns me, remind me that You are greater than my feelings. Reveal and silence any voices of shame or condemnation that are distorting my perspective of You and lead me to a deeper understanding and experience of Your love.

▶ DECLARE

God delights in forgiving my sins.

▶ ACT

Follow the example of Christ and forgive someone who has wronged you, asking God to give you joy as you do so.

Overcoming Unbelief

Immediately the boy's father exclaimed, "I do believe; help me overcome my unbelief!"

Mark 9:24 NIV

When you go through a season of doubt, it is easy to feel ashamed of your wavering faith. God, though, does not reject you when you doubt. Instead, He lovingly leads you back to belief.

The man who brought his demon-possessed son to Jesus (see Mark 9:17–26) was openly unsure about whether Jesus had the power to restore his son. "If you can do anything," he said, "take pity on us and help us" (v. 22 NIV). When Jesus noted his unbelief, the man didn't deny it, but in naked honesty, he begged Jesus to help him overcome his unbelief. Despite the man's imperfect faith, Jesus cast the evil spirit out of his son.

You can also be honest with Jesus about your doubts. You do not have to wear the smiling mask of "perfect faith" when your heart is breaking and your hope is wavering. Instead, you can re-member that Jesus Himself lived in human flesh and understands your heartache and limitations.

Lifting your eyes to Him and confessing your unbelief is actually a beautiful act of hope—saying, "Lord, I do not see things as they are, but oh, how I want to." He loves that kind of humble faith, and He will bless it.

▶ REFLECT

In what area am I struggling to believe God?

▶ PRAY

Father God, I am struggling to trust You. My doubts are shouting so loudly that they are drowning out the truth of Your Word. Although I may not *feel* hopeful right now, I lift my eyes to You in an *act* of hope, trusting that You will bring me to a place of renewed belief. I do believe. Help me overcome my unbelief.

▶ DECLARE

God helps my unbelief when I ask.

▶ ACT

Share with someone an area in which you are struggling to believe God and ask him or her to pray with you for renewed belief.

Equipped for Your Calling

"Now therefore go, and I will be with your mouth and teach you what you shall speak."

Exodus 4:12 ESV

God may call you to do things that incite fear, but He promises to equip you and go with you.

Like Moses, our insecurities may be preventing us from movement toward God's calling on our lives. We may feel inadequate to lead or even feel unable to speak. Despite Moses' inadequacies, God equipped him both to lead and to speak. He gave Moses instructions and affirmed His presence despite Moses' fears and insecurities.

God's power to equip you is already demonstrated through your unique makeup, gifts and talents. He also delights in showing His power through your weaknesses (see 2 Corinthians 4:7), so you can trust that God will move greatly in places where you feel inadequate. In both your strengths and your weaknesses, He has equipped you to move into His divine will, and He will be with you.

Movement with God begins with a first step. As Moses relied on God to speak, God filled his mouth, and He will do the same with you. When Moses spoke, miracles manifested.

What miracles might manifest when you move and speak as God commanded?

► **REFLECT**

What do I believe God has uniquely equipped me to do?

► **PRAY**

Father God, I submit my fears, insecurities and inadequacies to You. I surrender fully to Your will. I repent for every area of disobedience. I submit myself to Your goodwill and pleasure. God, help me to hope in You and in Your power. Help me to trust that You have equipped me for what You have asked me to do.

► **DECLARE**

God equips me to carry out His will.

► **ACT**

Identify one area in which God has asked and equipped you to move, then take one small step toward this calling.

19 | Hope in God's Covenant

"I will look on you with favor and make you fruitful and increase your numbers, and I will keep my covenant with you."

Leviticus 26:9 NIV

In this day and age, contracts are broken all the time. Can you really have hope in a covenant God made with you?

When you think of a person making a contract, what do you picture? A greedy salesman? A calculating lawyer? A scheming politician? These images can make it easy to discount the covenant God has made through Jesus. From a worldly standpoint, it often seems that contracts are made to be broken. In light of this, it can be easy to believe that God could also break a contract with us.

But when it comes to God, nothing could be further from the truth. Numbers 23:19 says, "God is not human, that he should lie, not a human being, that he should change his mind" (NIV). God can't break a promise. Lying is against His nature. He cannot do it!

God's covenant is not like a contract you sign with a bank. His covenant is a contract sealed with Jesus' blood. You can trust that God's covenant with you is unbreakable because He signed it with His blood, the irreversible payment for your sins.

► **REFLECT**

There are many covenant promises from God in the Bible. Which promise relates to my life circumstances, and how can I put my faith in it today?

► **PRAY**

Lord, I thank You for Your covenant promises. I may not have seen them come to pass yet, but I know You keep Your Word. All Your promises are "yes and amen" in Christ, and I can trust that since they were sealed with Jesus' blood, they are unbreakable.

► **DECLARE**

God fulfills His covenant promises to me.

► **ACT**

Following in Jesus' steps, fulfill a promise—big or small—that you have made to God or to someone else.

20 The God Who Hears

Let Your ear now be attentive and Your eyes open, to hear the prayer of Your servant which I am praying before You now, day and night, on behalf of the sons of Israel.

Nehemiah 1:6 NASB

When you cry out to God in times of distress, do you feel like He is listening or moving in response to your prayers?

Nehemiah cried out for God to hear him while he and his entire nation were in exile. Israel had been exiled for years, with only a small remnant still living in Jerusalem. Nehemiah opens his book by recounting the time when men returned to report on the state of a ransacked Jerusalem. He was so heartbroken to hear how the city had fallen into ruin that he fasted and wept for days.

After beseeching God to restore what had been lost, Nehemiah got up and went to work as the king's cupbearer. God was already moving. The king saw that Nehemiah was distressed and granted him permission to travel back to Jerusalem and begin reconstructing the city. This is nothing short of miraculous and could only have happened through God responding to His child's prayer.

Rest in the hope that God always hears. Sometimes He will answer no or ask you to wait. Other times He moves very quickly. But however He works, His heart is always for you.

▶ REFLECT

How has God shown that He hears me when I pray?

▶ PRAY

Father God, I know that Your timing and plans may look different from what I want, but I also know that when I come to You in prayer, You hear me. You always answer my prayers, and I can rest in the hope that You will move on my behalf.

▶ DECLARE

God hears my prayers.

▶ ACT

Write down an issue that has been burdening you and put it in a visible place. Whenever you see it, bring it to God in faith that He hears you.

21 God's Plan for Me

> "Now, my son, the LORD be with you, and may you have success and build the house of the LORD your God, as he said you would."
>
> 1 Chronicles 22:11 NIV

Think of the last big project you undertook. When you began, did you feel overwhelmed by its magnitude? God may call you to a project that feels impossible, but with Him, you have all that you need to succeed.

Solomon was tasked with the daunting, yet marvelous project of building God's Temple. He was a youth with no experience and no training. He did, however, have the only thing he needed to succeed. He had God's promise that his successful completion of the Temple was God's plan. Solomon was indeed successful in building the Temple, and it was considered one of the most spectacular buildings in the world at the time.

When God promises to equip us, that is all we need. Joshua 1:8 says that if we meditate on God's Word, our ways will be prosperous, and we will have good success. By focusing on God's Word and making it a part of our lives, our trust in this promise will flourish. No project will be too big. No plan will seem too complicated.

Imagine what God will do in your life if you have hope in His plan for you and step forward in faith.

▶ REFLECT

What plans do I believe God has called me to accomplish?

▶ PRAY

Lord, I thank You that You desire to give me success in Your plans for me. Help me to hide Your Word in my heart. I want to continue to meditate on Your Word so that You will make my way prosperous, and so that I will have good success. I have hope in Your plans for me.

▶ DECLARE

God fulfills His plans for me.

▶ ACT

Take one step toward completing a task you know God has directed you to do.

22 Hope for Spiritual Awakening

"And it shall come to pass afterward that I will pour out My Spirit on all flesh."

Joel 2:28 NKJV

God wants to pour out His Spirit upon you and those around you.

Stop and think about what this means. When God pours out His Spirit upon people, they typically begin to do supernatural things at His direction. In fact, every miracle in the Bible was performed by someone who had God's Spirit in operation upon, within or around him.

This truth is amazing, even hard to believe, but that is the good part. All you need to do is say, "Lord, pour out Your Spirit on me," then begin to walk forward with expectancy. God will begin to show you opportunities to walk with Him by His Holy Spirit. You will begin to see the world through His eyes, and you will start to feel His compassion well up within you, prompting you to become His hands and feet.

As you make this prayer a part of your daily lifestyle, you will begin to understand the reality of Jesus' promise in Matthew

28:20: "And lo, I am with you always, even to the end of the age" (NKJV).

As you walk close to Jesus with your ears attuned to the Holy Spirit, He will work through you in ways that go beyond what you imagine.

▶ REFLECT

What is the first thing I would do if I was certain that God's Spirit was poured out upon my flesh?

▶ PRAY

Father God, pour out Your Spirit upon me and lead me in ways of obedient service. Open my eyes to people's needs before they even open their mouths. Let my heart become sensitive to the Holy Spirit's promptings so that I may be Your hands and feet. Do things through me that would be impossible without Your Spirit.

▶ DECLARE

I receive the outpouring of God's Spirit.

▶ ACT

Pay close attention to the Holy Spirit's direction today, and respond to what He prompts you to do.

Release and Trust

> When she could hide him no longer, she took for him a basket made of bulrushes and daubed it with bitumen and pitch. She put the child in it and placed it among the reeds by the river bank.
>
> Exodus 2:3 ESV

Releasing something valuable and being unsure of the results can be overwhelming and heart-wrenching, but God is worthy of your trust.

The unknown is often agonizing and frightening. Releasing things to God can be especially difficult because we cannot always see His plans. Our only option is to trust. When Jochebed put her baby son, Moses, in a basket and watched him float down the river, she released her fear and trusted God to provide for her son.

Most of us would never trust God with such outcomes, hence the reason we see limited miracles. The parting of the Red Sea later happened because Jochebed had earlier released baby Moses into the water and trusted God with the total outcome.

When we struggle with releasing things to God, it demonstrates that something else other than God sits on the throne of our hearts. We also forfeit exceedingly precious promises because we will not release our hopes, our dreams and the control of our lives to God. God never asks us to release something without rewarding us in a greater measure. In fact, He takes pleasure in blessing His children (see Psalm 35:27).

If you are holding something back from God, release it! He will bless your faith in beautiful, unexpected ways.

▶ **REFLECT**

When have I had to release something valuable and trust God? What has been the outcome?

▶ **PRAY**

Father God, help me to release everything You ask me to release. Help me not to be possessive of the things with which You have blessed me. God, increase my trust in You, and help me to trust You with the unknown and all future outcomes. Empower me to trust that You know what is best for me.

▶ **DECLARE**

God works all things out for my good.

▶ **ACT**

Release to God something you have been holding on to, and share what you released with someone you trust.

24

Jesus' Perfect Empathy

> The Word became flesh and made his dwelling among us. We have
> seen his glory, the glory of the one and only Son, who came from
> the Father, full of grace and truth.
>
> John 1:14 NIV

When you are at your weakest, Jesus responds with overwhelming compassion. He perfectly empathizes with you because He Himself experienced the same weaknesses.

Hebrews 4:15 (NIV) says that Jesus "empathize[s] with our weaknesses . . . [and] has been tempted in every way, just as we are—yet he did not sin." In His mission to redeem you to eternal life, He did not discount the struggles that you would experience during your time in this fallen world. He chose to embody the same weak flesh that you inhabit, a finite house often clouded by hunger, cold and loneliness. He intimately empathizes with the draw of worldly desires because His flesh prickled with the same temptations you now fight. He, too, experienced physical pain—from backaches, to fatigue, to finally, veins that opened and leaked life away for your sake.

You never need to fear that your weakness will lessen God's love for you! It was out of His great love for you that He entered into the most vulnerable parts of the human experience. The One who redeemed you offers undying understanding because He once stood where you stand.

When you remember Jesus' perfect empathy, fear will retreat, and hope will take its rightful place.

▶ REFLECT

What weakness in my life can I consider through the lens of Jesus' empathy?

▶ PRAY

Jesus, how beautiful it is that You took on flesh and chose to face the same weaknesses that I now experience. Replace any despair I feel toward my weakness with a hope grounded in the truth of Your compassion, and fill me with a deeper understanding of Your intimate empathy and boundless love.

▶ DECLARE

Jesus is compassionate toward me.

▶ ACT

Consider a specific area of weakness in your life. Make the declaration above over that weakness. Then remind someone else of this truth today.

25 Hope in the Glory of God

> Through [Jesus] we have gained access by faith into this grace in which we now stand. And we boast in the hope of the glory of God.
>
> Romans 5:2 NIV

What is *glory*? To have hope in God's glory, it is important to understand exactly what it is.

According to Scripture, the glory of God is His invisible qualities displayed in a visible or knowable way. How has God made His invisible qualities visible? He did this through His Son, Jesus. Colossians 1:15 says that Jesus "is the image of the invisible God," and Hebrews 1:3 says, "He is the radiance of the glory of God and the exact imprint of his nature" (ESV).

When you hope in the glory of God, you are hoping in Jesus Himself. Jesus is not some invisible, intangible quality. He walked the earth. He performed miracles. He raised the dead. Most amazingly, He died for us, and the Father resurrected Him for our sake. The visible qualities Jesus displayed were shown so that we could have faith in the Father's invisible qualities. We can hope in God's glory because of Jesus, the only perfect image-bearer of God's glory.

As a follower of Jesus, you can be a conduit of God's glory as well. As you follow His commandments, He will use you to display His glory in the earth.

▶ REFLECT

What do I imagine when I think of God's glory?

▶ PRAY

Father God, I thank You for showing Your glory through the life of Jesus. As I reflect on Jesus' life and works, death and resurrection, I am thankful that You will do greater things through those of us who believe. Please let me be an instrument of Your glory in the earth.

▶ DECLARE

I am an image-bearer of God's glory.

▶ ACT

Do something today that showcases one of God's glorious qualities, such as showing His love or generosity to someone in need.

26 | Hope in God's Counsel

> You guide me with your counsel, and afterward you will take me
> into glory.
>
> Psalm 73:24 NIV

People often consult counselors when they need guidance, and
following their advice often produces good results. God, however, promises to guide you with *His* counsel. He is the perfect
Counselor, and following His instruction provides *great* results.

Who is the first person you run to when faced with a relational conflict, financial dilemma or big decision? You might run
to someone whom you consider wise, but even the greatest
wisdom falls short of God's. God's counsel is perfect in wisdom.
He sees what you cannot see because He is omnipresent and
omniscient, and because His eyes are not blurred by the lens of
sin. He has all the wisdom in the universe to bring to bear on
your issues, and He promises to give it freely and generously
when you ask.

God's counsel does not only guide you with perfect wisdom;
it also brings you comfort. Jesus said in John 14:26 that the Holy
Spirit, who is your Comforter, will teach you and remind you of
what Jesus has said. He will not leave you nor forsake you.

If you are faced with a seemingly hopeless dilemma, take heart! God has promised to give you perfect wisdom and comfort as you face today's trials.

▶ REFLECT

In what situation do I need God's counsel right now?

▶ PRAY

Lord, I thank You that You guide me with Your counsel and that You will bring me into glory. I trust You over all worldly counselors because Your counsel is sure. Thank You that as my Counselor, You bring comfort and wisdom to my circumstances and will lead me into all truth.

▶ DECLARE

I trust God's counsel.

▶ ACT

Set aside extended time to listen to the Holy Spirit today. Then share with someone else the counsel you feel you received.

Defeating Every Enemy

> Through God we will do valiantly, for it is he who will tread down
> our adversaries.
>
> Psalm 60:12 WEB

David wrote this psalm after experiencing difficulty defeating his enemies in battle. He had learned that only *through* and *with* God could he defeat every foe.

"Doing valiantly" is showing courage and determination to accomplish mighty things because you know God is fighting for you and with you.

So, the next time your Goliath seems too big to face, remember this: In the Garden of Eden, during the Flood and throughout the lives of the patriarchs and the prophets, God powerfully overcame His people's adversaries. From the virgin birth, through the life and the resurrection of Jesus and to your personal salvation, God has stepped powerfully into the lives of millions throughout history.

God also owns the future: The coming end-time events will be handled according to His plan, with you as an active, victorious participant. Romans 8:18 says, "What we suffer now is nothing compared to the glory he will reveal to us later" (NLT). The way we get to the glory God wants to reveal in us is to "do valiantly" through God in our difficulties.

Ask God what "doing valiantly" looks like for you today. Run with what the Holy Spirit brings to mind, and you will see Him trample down every adversary.

▶ REFLECT

In what area of my life can I "do valiantly" today through God's power?

▶ PRAY

God in heaven, reveal to me Your guiding hand. I acknowledge Your wisdom and Your presence in this moment. Help me acknowledge You in everything, so my ways can be made straight and filled with Your peace. I say right now, "You've got it, Lord," so I can be valiant in faith and confident in my hope in You.

▶ DECLARE

I will do valiantly today because God is with me.

▶ ACT

Take inventory of any enemies (real or perceived) that have been on your mind and ask the Holy Spirit what kind of valiant response He wants you to take.

28 God's Perfect Timing

> Pharaoh said to Joseph, "I hereby put you in charge of the entire
> land of Egypt." Then Pharaoh removed his signet ring from his
> hand and placed it on Joseph's finger.
>
> Genesis 41:41–42 NLT

When you are waiting, it can be hard to trust in God's timing, but you can be sure that His timing is *always* perfect.

We can all recall situations in which the timing seemed perfect. Everything aligned beautifully, mostly because we had a hand in orchestrating our circumstances. We can also remember the moments over which we had absolutely no control and how helpless or confused we felt in the moment.

Joseph, too, likely felt confused as to why God was allowing him to spend years in prison for a crime he did not commit (see Genesis 39–41). At just the right time, though, God raised Joseph up for a purpose that went far beyond what he had imagined.

Often, we try to create moments that only God can create. We network and share business cards, hoping to obtain what we think is best. However, only God can cause promotions, provide opportunities and open doors perfectly and in His perfect timing. God sometimes allows our efforts to fail because the timing is not right. He loves us too much to submit to our faulty timeline.

If you are still waiting, it does not mean that God has forgotten you, but that He is orchestrating the perfect timing for your life.

▶ REFLECT

In what area of my life do I need to trust God's perfect timing?

▶ PRAY

Father God, You are the Author and the Finisher of my faith. You are the Creator of time. You have promised to make everything beautiful in Your own time. Help me to remember that my times are in Your hands. Help me to release any doubt and trust in Your perfect timing.

▶ DECLARE

God's timing is perfect.

▶ ACT

Consider how you might act in an area in which you have been waiting for God's timing. Take a faith-filled step forward in prayer or a God-directed action of some kind.

29 Supernatural Confidence

> But the following night the Lord stood by him and said, "Be of good cheer, Paul; for as you have testified for Me in Jerusalem, so you must also bear witness at Rome."
>
> Acts 23:11 NKJV

Imagine being surrounded by an angry mob intent upon killing you without a second thought.

Many of us would have been terrified at the prospect of being surrendered to the mob and stoned or kept in Roman chains and ultimately led to a grisly death.

Yet despite these risks and the horrors the apostle Paul faced, he had a remarkable confidence in God. He had been there before, and he knew that Jesus was capable of delivering him from whatever scenario in which he found himself. And even if God did not deliver him, Paul had experienced enough of God's kindness and faithfulness to trust in His plan.

After overcoming the shock of seeing Jesus in our jail cell, many of us might have complained that despite this short-term good news, we were certain to meet our ultimate demise in Rome at the hands of Caesar. Yet, the knowledge of Jesus' supernatural and, at times, visible presence was all that Paul needed to press on toward a martyr's fate.

We may not presently be faced with such dramatic threats, yet Jesus' presence is as available to us as it was to Paul.

Whatever you face, you can have supernatural confidence in God's power and goodness.

▶ REFLECT

Where do I need supernatural confidence in God's power and goodness?

▶ PRAY

Father God, in whatever trials or conflicts I am facing, may I remember the ways that You acted in power and love on behalf of countless Christians before me. As I follow You, fill me with the same supernatural confidence that gave Paul boldness for You to the point of death.

▶ DECLARE

God gives me supernatural confidence.

▶ ACT

Reach out to someone who has exhibited supernatural confidence and ask him or her to share the things God has done to build this confidence in you.

30 Hope for Understanding

Daniel answered before the king and said, "As for the secret about which the king has inquired, neither wise men, sorcerers, soothsayer priests, nor diviners are able to declare it to the king. However, there is a God in heaven who reveals secrets."

Daniel 2:27–28 NASB

In Daniel 2, King Nebuchadnezzar summoned wise men from all over his kingdom and commanded them not only to interpret his disturbing recurring dream, but also to tell him exactly what he had dreamed. They could not, so Nebuchadnezzar ordered all of the wise men in the kingdom to be killed. Daniel then went before the Lord and asked for understanding, and the Lord answered with a vision of the king's dream.

When Daniel went before the king, he gave glory to God for revealing the truth of his dream. His accurate account and interpretation of the dream saved the lives of many people in Babylon. God did what every wise man in Babylon could not do; all Daniel had to do was ask.

God does not play cruel games with His children. When you ask for understanding, He may not give you every detail of the situation, but He will reveal exactly what you need to know. With God, you have hope of clarity and understanding.

▶ REFLECT

Where do I need God's understanding?

▶ PRAY

Lord, I trust that You love me and have my best interests at heart. Today, as I face things that feel confusing or foggy, please grant me understanding and peace. Show me the hidden things, so I can navigate this day with wisdom. Thank You for Your kindness and compassion in my life.

▶ DECLARE

Perfect understanding comes from God alone.

▶ ACT

In the center of a blank piece of paper, write a sentence or phrase that describes your situation. Then around that phrase, write out what the Holy Spirit reveals to you.

31 God's Motives Are Good

> "What does the LORD your God ask of you but to fear the LORD your God, to walk in obedience to him, to love him, to serve [him] . . . and to observe the LORD's commands and decrees that I am giving you today for your own good?"
>
> Deuteronomy 10:12–13 NIV

Following God's commands can feel like swimming upstream. If you feel discouraged as you strive to follow God, remember that He does not intend for His commands to be a burden, but a blessing.

The psalmist Asaph described his struggle with envy toward those who do not follow God's commands but seem to prosper (see Psalm 73). He reminded himself, though, that the prosperity of the wicked will be short-lived and that he has the lasting prosperity of intimacy with the God who is "good . . . to those who are pure in heart" (Psalm 73:1 NIV).

Each of God's commands is an overflow of His great love for you. When He tells you to fear and obey Him, He does not desire to constrain you, but to guide you to the only true Source of freedom. When He tells you to serve Him, He is inviting you to invest your energy in the only work that will truly satisfy.

When you choose to follow God's commands regardless of others' actions, you are exercising faith in God's good motives toward you. With your eyes fixed on God's goodness, you can walk in the path of God's commands energized by victorious hope.

▶ REFLECT

How has God shown me that His motives toward me are good?

▶ PRAY

Father God, I praise You that Your commands do not spring from a desire to restrict me, but to free me from the sin and darkness of this world. If there are any areas in which I have become weary in doing good, energize me to press on with a hope that is rooted in Your promises.

▶ DECLARE

God's motives toward me are always good.

▶ ACT

Choose one of God's commands and ask the Holy Spirit to help you to joyfully fulfill it today.

32 Hope in Jesus' Second Coming

> For the Lord Himself will descend from heaven with a shout, with the voice of an archangel, and with the trumpet of God. And the dead in Christ will rise first. Then we who are alive and remain shall be caught up together with them in the clouds to meet the Lord in the air. And thus, we shall always be with the Lord.
>
> 1 Thessalonians 4:16–17 NKJV

Have you ever reflected on the glorious truth that Jesus is truly coming back?

Take a moment to envision the events that are to come. As Jesus descends from His seat at the right hand of God the Father with a commanding shout, an archangel's voice is heard with the concurrent blast of a trumpet capable of being heard around the world.

Next, those who are in their graves are supernaturally summoned and rise from the dead. Not to be outdone, believers in Jesus still living their physical lives on the earth are caught up in the clouds in the twinkling of an eye (see 1 Corinthians 15:52) and meet Jesus in the air.

The Second Coming of Jesus has sustained millions of believers throughout the last two thousand years as they await the realization of the promises in Scripture. Although we do not know the day or the hour, Jesus wants us to live in hopeful preparation, confident that His Second Coming may very well happen in our lifetimes. May the truth that His return is close propel us to share the Good News with the lost and walk worthy of our calling.

Ready your heart and look toward the future with hope. Jesus is coming soon!

► **REFLECT**

How does the truth that Jesus may return in my lifetime affect my perspective on this earthly life?

► **PRAY**

Father God, help me begin to see my coming summons into Jesus' presence as inevitable as the rising of tomorrow's sun. Give me the faith to envision this great hope. And empower me to live this life with the certainty that I am guaranteed eternal life as I walk worthy of my calling as Your follower.

► **DECLARE**

Jesus is coming back soon.

► **ACT**

Use your imagination to envision these end-time scenarios with the same clarity as you recall your favorite film's climactic conclusion.

33 Words of Life

"It is the Spirit who gives life; the flesh is no help at all. The words that I have spoken to you are spirit and life."

John 6:63 ESV

Jesus said that His words are spirit and life. More than uttered sound, they carried supernatural ability and power. When you allow His words to remain in you, you can experience His life-giving power.

Jesus' words had spiritual power—they were able to restore life every time they emanated from His lips. His words also had significant psychological impact, unleashing God's power to heal mental illness and those persecuted by demons. When the disciples' words were unsuccessful, Jesus' words achieved the desired result. Jesus' words also had physical power. One word from Jesus, and shriveled limbs regrew, the blind received their sight and the chronically ill walked away whole.

God has given us the great gift of access to His Word. The apostle John exhorts us to ingest and be nourished by the Word, from the Old Testament prophecies of Christ's coming to Christ's glorious return in the book of Revelation.

The next time you open the Bible, praise God for this marvelous gift. As you abide in God's Word, its power will draw you closer to Christ in this life and give you hope for the life to come.

▶ REFLECT

What part of God's Word has affected my life the most?

▶ PRAY

Father God, help me to ingest Your Word so that I can become a garden that produces a harvest of Your spiritual fruit. Show me how to nurture these implanted words so that they grow without risk of crop failure. Help me to walk in light of these words so that I might reflect their truths in my daily interactions with others.

▶ DECLARE

God's Word abides within me.

▶ ACT

Reach out to someone who once shared God's Word with you and express your gratitude for his or her faithfulness.

34 A Door of Hope

> "There I will give her back her vineyards, and will make the Valley of Achor a door of hope. There she will respond as in the days of her youth, as in the day she came up out of Egypt."
>
> Hosea 2:15 NIV

When you're suffering in a mess of your own making, shame may whisper that God wants nothing to do with you. But the exact opposite is true: He is pursuing you with a fierce and unconditional love.

Hosea's pursuit of his wife, Gomer, is a striking analogy that points to God's relentless love for His children. Gomer was repeatedly unfaithful, running off to other men although her faithful husband loved her and provided for her. In the midst of Gomer's unfaithfulness, Hosea prophesied that God would make the Valley of Achor, which means "trouble," into a door of hope.

Following God's instructions, Hosea pursued Gomer, speaking words of love and tenderness, beckoning her to come home (see Hosea 3). Although Gomer was responsible for the mess in which she found herself, Hosea offered the love that could transform her mess into the beginning of a beautiful new life. In the same way, God wants to transform the trouble that we ourselves have caused into a door of hope.

When you fall, picture Jesus running to you, taking your hand and helping you to your feet. Refuse to walk away from Him out of shame; instead, walk confidently through the door of hope that He has provided.

▶ REFLECT

What trouble or sin of mine does God want to transform into a door of hope?

▶ PRAY

Gracious Savior, there is nothing I have done or will ever do that will separate me from Your love. Every time I fall, You lift me up, and every time I run away, You woo me back with Your love and faithfulness. With confidence in Your love, I choose to walk through the door of hope.

▶ DECLARE

God is opening a door of hope for me.

▶ ACT

Reflect on a time when God turned what the enemy meant for evil into good, and share this with someone who needs this message of hope.

35 Seeing through Spiritual Eyes

Now faith is confidence in what we hope for and assurance about what we do not see.

Hebrews 11:1 NIV

When seen through human eyes, things can look hopeless. But when viewed through spiritual eyes, the unshakable truth of God's promises comes into view. When you choose to look at your situation through spiritual eyes, you exchange your despair for confident hope.

Why do we need confidence in what we hope for? Many times, hope may seem like a waste of time and energy. The more we hope, the bleaker the situation appears to our naked eyes. If hope is to become active in our lives, we must look at our problems through spiritual eyes. Our spiritual eyes will see through our circumstances, the lies of Satan and the lies we tell ourselves.

Hebrews 11, often called "the Hall of Faith" chapter, builds us up with its many accounts of past believers' confidence in God, even when they could not see. Though Abraham couldn't see how he could become a father, he believed in God's promise and became a father at the age of one hundred. Though marching around the walls of Jericho seven times made no rational sense, the Israelites obeyed, and the city walls fell. All of those mentioned in Hebrews 11 share a common characteristic: They chose to see through spiritual eyes.

What can you see with your spiritual eyes? Gaze on that instead of your circumstances!

▶ REFLECT

What invisible reality do I confidently see with my spiritual eyes?

▶ PRAY

Holy Spirit, open my spiritual eyes. Help me to have confidence and hope in Your promises even when I cannot see. Increase my faith to withstand the fiery darts of Satan that come to steal my hope in Your promises. Lord, help me to remember that You cannot lie. God, right now increase my hope, trust and faith in You alone.

▶ DECLARE

My spiritual eyes see how God sees.

▶ ACT

Reframe a trial you are facing by looking at it through spiritual eyes.

36 King Jesus, Our Hope

> Paul, an apostle of Jesus Christ, by the commandment of God our
> Savior and the Lord Jesus Christ, our hope.
>
> 1 Timothy 1:1 NKJV

Have you reflected on who Jesus is beyond being the sacrifice for
sin? Because of the weight of the cross, it is easy to forget that not
only did He sacrifice Himself, but He is eternally King!

Not only was Jesus the hope of Israel, but He was the hope of the
entire world. He laid down His life for us at Calvary, arose three days
later and is now seated at the right hand of God the Father in heaven.

If you could revisit the apostle Paul's revelations (see 2 Corinthians 12:2), you would fully understand what it means that Jesus
is the image of the invisible God.

Jesus is the firstborn over all creation because He is the Creator of all things, visible and invisible. All things were created
through Him and ultimately for Him. As a result, He is before all
things, and in Him all things consist. Because He is the beginning
and the firstborn from the dead, in all things He is superior to all
others (see Colossians 1:15–18).

Remember that not only is Jesus the suffering sacrifice at Calvary, but He is the risen King of the created realms whose blood
has secured eternal life for you in heaven with Him.

▶ REFLECT

How is the kingship of Jesus represented in my life?

▶ PRAY

King Jesus, help me to see You anew through the eyes of the prophets and the apostles so that I, too, may have their fervent hope. Help me trace each mention of Your role in my redemption from Genesis through Revelation so I can see the full picture of who You are.

▶ DECLARE

Jesus is my King.

▶ ACT

Do one thing in service of King Jesus today that reflects His humble, selfless sacrifice.

37 God's Perfect Promises

"Behold, I am with you and will keep you wherever you go, and will bring you back to this land. For I will not leave you until I have done what I have promised you."

Genesis 28:15 ESV

God wants you to have everything He promised.

Have you ever doubted God? It is easy to lose hope in God's promises because of elongated time lapses, life-altering circumstances and our frustrations with life. At times they can make God's promises seem like lies. However, none of these things can hinder God's decrees. In fact, God promises never to leave us or forsake us. What a commitment! Most people have heard the saying "Promises are made to be broken," but this is not so with God.

A perfect promise is without fault or defect; it is absolutely complete. God is absolutely perfect, and everything He does is perfect (see Psalm 18:30). It is impossible for Him to lie (see Numbers 23:19). Hoping in a perfect God who does everything perfectly guarantees fulfilled promises. People and things may leave your life, but God never will. He will do exactly what He promised you He would do.

A perfect God has crafted perfect promises for you. So, then, why would you doubt? Focus on God's promises to you and incline your ears to His voice. God will perfect every promise He has made.

▶ **REFLECT**

Where do I need to reignite my hope in God's promises to me?

▶ **PRAY**

Father God, I lay aside everything that keeps me in doubt. Help me to remember Your perfect faithfulness. Lord, You cannot lie, and You have not lied to me. Help me to remember that all of Your promises are "yes and amen." God, You will do exactly as You have said.

▶ **DECLARE**

God always fulfills His promises.

▶ **ACT**

Fulfill a promise you have made to yourself, your spouse, a child or a friend today.

38 Every Prophecy Fulfilled

For the law made nothing perfect; on the other hand, there is the bringing in of a better hope, through which we draw near to God.

Hebrews 7:19 NKJV

Did you know that Jesus fulfilled over 350 identifiable Old Testament prophecies that clearly showed He was the Messiah?

Israel's Messiah was foretold in Old Testament prophecy thousands of years before Jesus' arrival as a babe in Bethlehem. The Messiah was expected to fulfill these prophecies and to deliver Israel from its oppressors, like His physical and spiritual ancestor King David (see Luke 1:32–34).

Although Jesus did not come as the earthly warrior the Israelites expected, He fulfilled each Old Testament prophecy with precision and eternal glory beyond what His people could have imagined.

Jesus also laid the foundation for a New Covenant, defined by its better promises (see Hebrews 8:6), and He uttered new prophecies of an eternity with God for His followers, complete with an end to sorrow and gold-paved streets (see Revelation 21:21).

When we assemble all the evidence surrounding Jesus' earthly life against the backdrop of prophecy found throughout the Old

Testament, we begin to see a glimpse of the magnitude of the God revealed throughout the Bible.

Since God has shown a perfect track record of fulfilling His prophetic words, you can trust that every New Testament promise and prophecy will be fulfilled beyond your ability to imagine (see Ephesians 3:20).

▶ **REFLECT**

If God is the same yesterday, today and forever, what does that mean for me and my walk with Him?

▶ **PRAY**

Father, I praise You for fulfilling each prophecy You gave about Jesus. May these fulfilled words point me to Your faithfulness so I may hope in Your ability to fulfill the prophecies of things to come. Let me become increasingly aware of the unshakable nature of Your promises so I can walk with ever-increasing confidence in You.

▶ **DECLARE**

God fulfills every prophecy.

▶ **ACT**

Search the internet for "prophecies Jesus fulfilled" and highlight some of them in your Bible.

39 A Well-Watered Tree

"But blessed is the one who trusts in the LORD, whose confidence is in him. They will be like a tree planted by the water that sends out its roots by the stream. It does not fear when heat comes; its leaves are always green."

Jeremiah 17:7–8 NIV

It is easy to idolize the people in your life, expecting them to meet your deepest needs and being disappointed when they don't. When you put your confidence in God, though, He will never fail to satisfy you.

Scripture describes those who trust in others for their strength as a bush in the wastelands, desperate for water to quench their thirst but rooting themselves far from the source of true satisfaction (see Jeremiah 17:5–6). When we look to others to meet our deepest needs, we, too, are clinging to what can never satisfy.

The only One who can satisfy us is our Creator, who knows our frames because He was the One who knitted them together. He knows what will fulfill our deepest longings because He was the One who put those desires in our hearts in the first place.

Do not put your trust in humans, who are as frail and finite as you. Instead, trust in the God of infinite strength who created you.

When you put your hope in humans, they will never quench your thirst. But when you put your hope in God, He will transform you into a well-watered, flourishing tree.

▶ REFLECT

In what areas have I been trusting in other people rather than in God?

▶ PRAY

Father God, I confess that I have often looked to others for strength rather than to You. You are the ultimate Source of strength and satisfaction, and I long to know You better! Show me what it means to be satisfied in You—transform me from a bush in the wastelands into a well-watered, flourishing tree.

▶ DECLARE

When I trust in God, I am like a well-watered tree.

▶ ACT

Put a copy of Jeremiah 17:7–8 in a place where you are often tempted to trust in others for strength and satisfaction.

40 Stepping into Miracles

And Peter answered him, "Lord, if it is you, command me to come to you on the water."

Matthew 14:28 ESV

Walking on water defies all the laws of nature, yet Jesus empowered Peter to do it. God wants *you* to walk on water, too.

We can do everything God commands us to do. But faith and hope are prerequisites for these water-walking experiences. Doubt and fear hinder us from walking on water. What could we really do if we turned a blind eye and a deaf ear to doubt and fear?

There were others in the boat with Peter, but only Peter walked on the water. How many opportunities do we miss out on due to our fear, remaining content with watching others do what God commanded? God wants people who are full of faith and hope to accomplish great things for Him. We can do everything our Lord commands us to do if our eyes are fixed on Him rather than on the raging winds, the blazing inferno or anything else that beckons us to take our eyes off of God.

Answer Jesus' call and step into the miracles that are right in front of you. Keep your eyes on Him, and you will walk on water.

► **REFLECT**

What "water-walking" steps is God beckoning me to take?

► **PRAY**

Father God, I thank You for faith to walk on water. I thank You that I can do everything You command me to do through the power of the Spirit. Thank You for the miracles that await my obedience. Thank You for reminders that You want me to follow Your leading. Father, may I not be hindered by fear and doubt. They are powerless over me.

► **DECLARE**

I can do everything God commands me to do.

► **ACT**

Take one step "out upon the waters" that you have been putting off out of fear.

Hope for Justice

> How long, LORD, have I called for help, and You do not hear? I cry
> out to You, "Violence!" Yet You do not save.
>
> Habakkuk 1:2 NASB

Have you ever looked at our world and wondered if God is missing the evening news? Does it feel like He is letting things slide, or that He just does not care about this issue or that injustice?

Habakkuk started off with a bold complaint: "How long have I called for help?" He asked God to vindicate the people of Israel, but God did not seem to respond. Habakkuk even asked for violence against God's enemies. In the same way we cry out for God to stop the darkness of our day, God's prophet was crying out for reinforcements that did not seem to be coming.

As we witness injustice, it is easy to ask, "Are you seeing this, God?" He is. Nothing escapes His gaze, and every person will give an account for their actions. While it may look like the window for justice is closing, God is never late. His justice is perfect. We cannot orchestrate or imagine the fullness of His justice because we cannot see the end of the story.

As you encounter injustices, remember who is the ultimate Judge. He has not laid down His gavel, He is not asleep and He will not ignore His children.

► REFLECT

Where do I want to see God's justice in my life?

► PRAY

Lord, You are a righteous judge. As I witness injustice in my own life and in my world, I bring the cries of my heart before You with the hope and faith that You will pass perfect judgment. You do not miss anything, and I trust You with this situation.

► DECLARE

God's justice never fails.

► ACT

Talk with someone about an injustice that is pressing on your heart and pray about a role God might have you play in righting that wrong.

42 Salvation for My Household

> The jailer brought them into his house and set a meal before them;
> he was filled with joy because he had come to believe in God—he
> and his whole household.
>
> Acts 16:34 NIV

When you come to know Jesus but your family does not immediately follow, it can be easy to fear that God is not working on them. Rest assured: There is hope for your loved ones!

You can trust that God fervently desires a relationship with your family members. However much you love them, He loves them infinitely more. He wants them to live, not die, and He will pursue them just as He pursued you (see 2 Peter 3:9).

God has a way of reaching an entire household. In Acts 10, when Peter preached the Gospel at Cornelius's house, the entire household was saved. In Acts 16, the Philippian jailer who was guarding Paul and Silas in prison received the Lord—with his whole family. In the same way, God has the power to save your entire household, no matter how resistant they have been or how long you have prayed without seeing any change of heart.

Keep praying, keep speaking the truth, and keep reflecting Jesus in your actions. Most importantly, though, keep trusting in

God's love for your family members and believe that He wants everyone in your household to be saved.

▶ **REFLECT**

Which of my immediate or extended family members do not yet know Jesus as Savior and Lord?

▶ **PRAY**

Lord, I thank You that You desire that none would perish but that all would spend eternity with You. I ask for the Holy Spirit to open the spiritual eyes of my family members, that they would know the hope to which they have been called. Bring them into Your family, and use me in the process.

▶ **DECLARE**

God wants my entire household to be saved!

▶ **ACT**

Reach out to someone in your family who is not yet a follower of Jesus and bless him or her in some way. Allow the Holy Spirit to guide your interactions with that person.

43 A Second Chance

> Yet for love's sake I rather appeal to you . . . I appeal to you for my son Onesimus . . . who once was unprofitable to you, but now is profitable to you and to me.
>
> Philemon 1:9–11 NKJV

Have you ever been given a second chance, even if you did not deserve it?

At one point, Onesimus had fallen beneath Paul and Philemon's expectations. However, Paul asked that renewed confidence be given to Onesimus so that he could fulfill his original potential and be of benefit to Paul, Philemon and Onesimus himself.

Is not this second chance illustrative of Jesus' love for us? Despite our multiple failures, Jesus, by His Holy Spirit, reaches out to us daily with the message that we can return to Him without condemnation.

Paul himself was ever mindful of his earlier days, when he persecuted the emerging Church. In his dealings with Onesimus, we can see that the grace Jesus offered him forever impacted his willingness to believe the best and restore others so that they might fulfill God's calling on their lives.

Jesus' work on the cross has made it possible for the righteous Judge of the universe to be the God of second chances. Paul was merely following Jesus' example and giving Onesimus an illustration of the power of God's grace and forgiveness.

No matter how many times you have messed up, God offers you the chance to start again.

▶ **REFLECT**

When I received a second chance, what was my emotional response?

▶ **PRAY**

Father God, I thank You that through the power of Jesus' sacrifice, I have been given the greatest possible second chance. I know that I fall short in many ways, and I thank You that when I stumble, You are always there to help me up. May I treat others with the same grace You have lavished on me.

▶ **DECLARE**

God gives me another chance.

▶ **ACT**

Follow the Holy Spirit and extend forgiveness, mercy and another chance to someone who has wronged you.

44 Weapons of Hope

> Why are you cast down, O my soul, and why are you in turmoil within me? Hope in God; for I shall again praise him, my salvation and my God.
>
> Psalm 42:11 ESV

Inner turmoil can be very real and hard to manage. Nevertheless, God offers you hope amid turmoil through the weapons of praise and thanksgiving.

When we are feeling down, we can always find reasons to praise God. If we feel threatened by our circumstances, God grants us the weapon of praise. It is difficult to remain downcast when you practice thanksgiving. Giving thanks to God allows Him to be the lifter of our heads. Being down and out does not mean it is over. Being down is temporary, and better days are on the horizon. Praise makes things more pleasant in the meantime.

Defeat is often deceptive, and it wants us to come in agreement with it. We must remember that in Christ, we are already more than conquerors (see Romans 8:37). King David reminded us that sometimes we have to encourage ourselves. His hope was not automatic; he had to tell his soul to "hope in God"!

The encouraging words you need are already inside of you. What do you need to tell yourself in your sadness and turmoil?

Sadness is a feeling, but hope involves action. Encourage yourself in the Lord through praise and thanksgiving.

▶ REFLECT

Where do I need to praise God as an act of hope?

▶ PRAY

Father God, thank You that sadness is temporary. Thank You that You have given me the power of life in my tongue, that through my words I can encourage myself in the Lord. God, help me to remember that I can praise You even when things are tough. Thank You, Lord, that I can hope in You.

▶ DECLARE

Praise and thanksgiving are my weapons of hope.

▶ ACT

As often as possible today, express your gratitude to God and others.

45 | God Sees You

Behold, the eye of the Lord is on those who fear Him, on those who wait for His faithfulness.

Psalm 33:18 NASB

Do you believe God sees you? Do you believe His eye has swept over you once or twice in a passing glance, or does He watch you lovingly as a father watches over his child?

God is omnipotent, and He watches over all His creation, but He watches His children a little differently. In the same way a parent on a crowded playground can spot her own child among many children, God's gaze pursues those who call Him Lord. He is near to those who honor, fear and rely on Him, and He keeps close by to supply protection and provision.

God sees you. He knows your needs, your fears and your desires. He knows what every day of your life will look like. He has seen you at your most heartbroken and at your happiest. Not only does He see you, but He longs to be near you.

Whatever you are facing today, be it joyful or challenging, know that you are seen and known. You have hope because your Father desires to be close and to keep you in His protective, loving sight.

▶ REFLECT

Have I ever felt like God didn't see me?

▶ PRAY

Thank You for seeing me, Father. Thank You for knowing my desires and my struggles. I am blessed to be called Your child and to be safe under Your gaze. There is nowhere I can go where You will lose sight of me, and Your protective hand follows me always.

▶ DECLARE

The loving eye of the Lord is upon me.

▶ ACT

Identify a time or event in your life when you felt God's attention, and share this testimony with someone.

46 Hope against All Hope

> Against all hope, Abraham in hope believed and so became the father of many nations, just as it had been said to him, "So shall your offspring be."
>
> Romans 4:18 NIV

When you are powerless to change your situation, you may feel imprisoned in a cell of hopelessness. The key to your freedom is not a change in circumstances, but hope in the God who is not bound by circumstances.

Abraham had no power to change his situation. Although God had promised him a son, at seventy-five years old with an aging wife, Abraham knew the fulfillment of God's promise was humanly impossible. His firm hope seems laughable to a world that views life in terms of human ability. It was against this narrow, worldly hope that Abraham hoped, and he was not disappointed. Sarah bore Isaac twenty-five years later at ninety years old, testifying that God's promises are not constrained by human limits.

Your circumstances do not constrain what God can and will do in your life. When you hope against all hope as Abraham did, you are hoping against a brittle, worldly hope that crumbles at the sight of God's promises. As a Christian, you are not bound by the laws of this world but freed by the power of Christ.

Today, choose to hope against all hope. Watch and be amazed as God's power transcends your circumstances, for His promises never fail.

▶ REFLECT

Where do I need to exercise hope that transcends my circumstances?

▶ PRAY

God of Abraham, how wonderful it is that Your power and promises are not constrained by the limits of this world. As Abraham did, I want to choose to hope against all hope. If I have been limiting my hope to my own abilities, help me lift my eyes to hope in You, the All-Powerful God, who always fulfills Your promises.

▶ DECLARE

Against all hope, in hope I believe.

▶ ACT

Listen to the Holy Spirit and take a step of faith toward something you have felt hopeless about in the past.

Hope for Discernment

"So give your servant a discerning heart to govern your people and to distinguish between right and wrong. For who is able to govern this great people of yours?"

1 Kings 3:9 NIV

When faced with difficult decisions, have you ever felt that God has given you too much to handle? As a believer, you can exchange your heavy burden for hope—God promises to give discernment generously when you ask.

Young King Solomon was also faced with more than he could handle. The task ahead was overwhelming, and he knew that in order to govern God's people, he needed a wise and understanding heart. God loved Solomon's humble request, and He blessed it abundantly, lavishing wisdom on him so he could fulfill his purpose.

When you lack understanding, when you are overwhelmed by indecision, cry out to God just as Solomon did. Take heart and wait in hope that God will also fill you with the discernment you need to take confident action. This hope for wisdom is much more than wishful thinking—God has said multiple times in His Word not only that He gives wisdom, but that wisdom is a gift He *loves* to give!

What you are facing may be more than you can handle, but it is not more than He can handle. He has promised to walk with you in every decision, guiding and teaching you as you look to Him.

▶ REFLECT

In what area do I need to ask and believe God for discernment?

▶ PRAY

God of all understanding, I thank You that You give wisdom generously to me when I ask. I desperately need Your discernment to handle the decisions and questions before me. Help me to rest from striving to devise my own solutions and empower me to wait in confident hope for the wisdom You have promised to give.

▶ DECLARE

God delights to give me discernment.

▶ ACT

Write down a prayer for discernment in a specific area, keep it in a visible place, and wait in hope for God's answer.

48 Judgment Removed

> Who is a God like You, who pardons wrongdoing and passes over a rebellious act of the remnant of His possession? He does not retain His anger forever, because He delights in mercy.
>
> Micah 7:18 NASB

As you have considered your past failings, have you ever feared that some of your sins are beyond forgiveness?

God is perfectly holy. He is so holy that when Jesus took the sins of the world upon His own body, God the Father looked away. God is also perfectly just. When we read passages where God executes judgment on a corrupt person or nation, part of us may rejoice to see justice served.

What happens, though, when we examine our own lives through that same lens of justice? What do we feel when we see our own wickedness in comparison with God's holiness? As we recall the sins that have tainted our lives, we may slip into believing that some of them are beyond forgiveness. We may even believe that we still deserve judgment for the things we have done.

First John 1:9 (NIV) says, "If we confess our sins, he is faithful and just and will forgive us our sins and purify us from all unrighteousness." God promises that while there are some natural consequences that occur as a result of sin, His wrath has turned from you. You have a hope of eternity with Him because of the mercy of God.

► REFLECT

Where do I believe I have trespassed beyond mercy and am deserving of judgment?

► PRAY

Lord, help me to believe that when You say my sins are wiped away and You do not remember them, I am forgiven because of what Jesus has done. I am loved and completely absolved by His blood. Thank You for forgiving me and for removing Your judgment from me.

► DECLARE

God removes all judgment against me when I repent.

► ACT

Call to mind a time when someone forgave you, and send him or her a message of gratitude for giving you a window into God's mercy and forgiveness.

49 The Friendship of the Holy Spirit

"And I will ask the Father and he will give you another Savior, the Holy Spirit of Truth, who will be to you a friend just like me—and he will never leave you. . . . You know him intimately, because he remains with you and will live inside you."

John 14:16–17 TPT

How would you describe your closest friends? Are they trustworthy? Wise? Compassionate? As a believer, you can embrace the marvelous hope that the Holy Spirit is your friend!

Shortly before Jesus was crucified, He promised His twelve disciples that the Father would send the Holy Spirit in His stead when He returned to heaven. The disciples did not need to despair at Jesus' departure, for He had given them hope for the intimate communion with God they all longed for. What's more, Jesus imparted this hope: The Holy Spirit would be the most faithful of friends, not only to the Twelve, but to all believers.

The friendship of the Holy Spirit is unique: Not only does He comfort you, but He lives *in* you (see 1 Corinthians 3:16). Not only does He advise you, but He does so *perfectly*. Not only does

He nourish you, but He produces fruit in you that will nourish others.

You can face the most challenging of days with great hope when you embrace the intimate friendship of the Holy Spirit. As you remember His friendship, you can face the day with steadiness, knowing that He will guide you, comfort you and never leave you.

▶ REFLECT

How has the Holy Spirit shown Himself to be my friend?

▶ PRAY

Holy Spirit, thank You for Your friendship! How marvelous it is that You not only comfort and teach me, but that You also live within me. Guide me with Your wisdom and clarity in my interactions and decisions today. Produce fruit in me so that others might see Your glory and also know Your friendship.

▶ DECLARE

The Holy Spirit is my close friend.

▶ ACT

Make a mental or written list of what is most important to you in a friend. Then consider how the Holy Spirit exemplifies these characteristics.

50 Hope for a Righteous Ruler

Of the increase of His government and peace there will be no end, upon the throne of David and over His kingdom, to order it and establish it with judgment and justice from that time forward, even forever. The zeal of the LORD of hosts will perform this.

Isaiah 9:7 NKJV

It may seem odd to feel excitement when you hear a verse about the increasing size of a government.

Even the most successful governments in history were weakened by the greed, pride and abuse of unrighteous leaders. Of the great governments to rise upon the earth, all reached their zenith and then slowly crumbled into antiquity. Yet the Scripture above foretells that Jesus' righteous government will not only cover the earth to the exclusion of all others, but it will also continue to expand outward until His reign covers the entire created realm.

As a joint heir with Jesus (see Romans 8:17), you are a part of this righteous government and a member of the heavenly royal family. Although this may be difficult to understand, this truth gives birth to a hope that reaches far beyond this lifetime.

Imagine yourself working for Jesus, the only perfectly righteous ruler, helping Him increase His government as He sits as King on a supernatural throne for all eternity.

It may sound too good to be true, but this is an indisputable promise of God: Jesus' righteous reign is the future of all who have made Jesus Lord of their lives.

▶ REFLECT

How has Jesus shown Himself to be a righteous ruler in my life?

▶ PRAY

Holy Spirit, open my eyes to the wonders of the righteous government that King Jesus will rule in the infinite ages to come. Give me revelation of the nature of Your righteous government, so my faith can rise to see it, as Your prophet Isaiah did thousands of years ago.

▶ DECLARE

I will rule and reign with Jesus in His righteous Kingdom.

▶ ACT

Write down as many things as you can that would typify a Jesus-ruled government versus the characteristics you see in present earthly governments.

51 God's Help in Trouble

God is our refuge and strength, a very present help in trouble.

Psalm 46:1 NKJV

Have you ever been outside in the heat of summer, parched and longing for a cool drink, when suddenly, as if on cue, a cool breeze comes out of nowhere and refreshes you?

At times, it may seem as if God has dispatched the ideal breeze just for you. The invisible God of Scripture is always there, closer than your breath (see Romans 10:8). The mere whisper of His name invites His presence to meet you right where you are in that very moment, with exactly what you need to feel relief amid trouble.

As David wrote in his psalm, God is a very present help. In fact, as we begin to gain confidence in His being "present," we realize to an increasing degree that He can serve as a refuge spiritually and psychologically, and He even keeps us from physical harm.

As you learn to rely on this place of refuge, you can develop a resilient strength that empowers you to stand strong despite your present circumstances. This strength can empower you to overcome setbacks, disappointments and even overt failure. Such strength gives you the ability to ask, seek and knock until God's deliverance comes to pass.

▶ **REFLECT**

If I could see God in all His majestic power and strength hovering over me right now, how would that change how I feel about my current situation?

▶ **PRAY**

Father God, I invite Your presence to be with me now. Thank You for Your promise to never leave me nor forsake me. I look beyond the seen realm to acknowledge You as my refuge and strength. As I put my trust in You, I look forward to seeing Your deliverance as my spiritual forefathers did so long ago.

▶ **DECLARE**

God is my refuge and strength in every situation.

▶ **ACT**

Make a list of every time God has delivered you from trouble or potential failure. Use this list as the beginning of a "Testimonies List," which you can update and be encouraged by as you trust God in times of trouble.

52 Made for Friendship

And Jonathan made David vow again because of his love for him,
because he loved him as he loved his own life.

1 Samuel 20:17 NASB

In a world of constant yet shallow connections, who are your
true friends? Do you sometimes feel surrounded by people, but
very much alone?

In this section of 1 Samuel, the two most famous friends in the
Bible were in the middle of a weighty conflict. David discovered
King Saul had set a trap to have him killed in the palace, so he
went to Saul's son Jonathan. Jonathan loved David to the point
that he sided against his own father and king to secure David's
safety. He then made David enter into a covenant of friendship
not once, but twice.

Even in the midst of danger and Saul's betrayal, these two
friends embodied a healthy, sacrificial friendship. They are living
proof that God designed us to walk side by side with like-minded
believers who love and refine us. God speaks about friendship
dozens of times in the Scriptures because it matters so much
to Him. We were never meant to be lone wolves, especially in
times of trial.

God cares about your relationships. He is your greatest Friend, but He also created you for deep and meaningful friendships with other people. He will be faithful to provide the friends that you need.

▶ **REFLECT**

Who in my life do I consider a true friend?

▶ **PRAY**

Father, You created me to be in community and to have good, healthy friendships that sharpen me and draw me toward Your heart. You are my greatest Friend, but earthly friendships are so important too. I ask that You continue to surround me with friends who love You, love me and point me back to Jesus.

▶ **DECLARE**

I have been created for healthy friendships.

▶ **ACT**

Send an encouraging note to someone whom you consider a true friend. If you do not have someone like this, ask the Lord to bring a true friend into your life.

53 Hope That Acts

After they had heard the king, they went on their way, and the star they had seen when it rose went ahead of them until it stopped over the place where the child was. When they saw the star, they were overjoyed.

Matthew 2:9–10 NIV

The Christian life can be a great adventure! Jesus calls you to the exciting task of proclaiming His love and glory to a dark world. A powerful way to do this is to *act* on the hope you have.

A great example of active hope is the account of the Magi (see Matthew 2:1–12). When they saw the star that declared Jesus' birth, they excitedly set out on the journey to find the long-awaited Savior. Although their journey was lengthy and arduous, they were refreshed by great joy when their hope was fulfilled.

In the same way, you can joyfully act on the hope you have because God always fulfills His promises. When you share His Word, you can be sure it will not return void. When you are persecuted for your faith, you can be sure of God's favor. When you trust Him for what you need, you can be sure He will provide.

Acting in hope is not always easy, but it is always worth it. Just as the Magi did, you can expect that God will refresh you with joy on the journey. How will you act on the hope that you have?

► **REFLECT**

Where is God calling me to act on my hope?

► **PRAY**

God of all hope, empower me to follow the example of the Magi so that I may act on the great hope that I have in You. Bring to mind specific things I can do to both proclaim and live out Your Word. As I act, fill me with great joy in Your goodness and love.

► **DECLARE**

God blesses my active hope.

► **ACT**

Act in faith and hope on something God is showing you today.

54 Peace with God

Therefore, since we have been justified through faith, we have peace with God through our Lord Jesus Christ.

Romans 5:1 NIV

Everyone longs for relational peace, but in a fallen world, this type of peace is often elusive. Through Jesus Christ, though, you have the greatest kind of peace—peace with God!

We especially desire relational peace with our families. We want to feel connected, and anything that separates us from family members is painful. You may know of people who no longer relate to members of their family because of past hurt. There is no peace in those situations.

God wanted a family, but sin separated humanity from Him. There was no peace between God and man. Through Jesus' death and resurrection, however, He made a way for us to be reunited with our heavenly Father. By grace through faith, we now have peace with God.

You now can have a relationship with your heavenly Father, for there is no more separation. You can have close fellowship with a Father who wants to know everything about you—your deepest desires and your biggest concerns, your highs and your lows. He is a good Father, and you can rest in Him.

Since you now have peace with Him through faith in Jesus, you can rejoice in being a member of God's family!

▶ **REFLECT**

Where has God brought relational peace into my life because of His presence?

▶ **PRAY**

Father, I thank You that I have peace with You. Thank You that I can have an intimate relationship and share my deepest desires with You! May I be filled with an awareness of Your closeness as I face the day. You are a good Father, and I am grateful I am Your child.

▶ **DECLARE**

I have peace with God through faith in Jesus.

▶ **ACT**

Find a person you have an issue with or who has an issue with you and make peace with him or her today.

55 Deferred Hopes

> And in due time Hannah conceived and bore a son, and she called his name Samuel, for she said, "I have asked for him from the LORD."
>
> 1 Samuel 1:20 ESV

God wants you to bring your desperate desires to Him.

Children's desires for things are often accompanied with cries of distress and bitter weeping. Deep desires can cause us, too, to respond in desperation. Misdirected desperation can bring devastating consequences, but when we submit our desires to the Lord, we can trust that He will answer.

Have you ever witnessed someone turn to God in desperation for a desire to be fulfilled? Have you ever cried out to the Lord in agony? Many women have cried out to God in desperation because of a barren womb, like Hannah. Hannah promised that if He would but grant her a son, she would offer him to God's service. God answered Hannah's cry by giving her Samuel.

God is moved with compassion and answers our prayers when we seek Him. He sees our tears and sacrifice. He desires that we submit our deep, desperate needs to His care, and He will answer them in His way and in His timing, which is always best.

Demonstrate your hope in God by turning to Him in desperation for your heart's desire, for He takes pleasure in responding to your cries.

▶ REFLECT

What deferred hopes do I have and need to give to Jesus?

▶ PRAY

Father God, when my hope is deferred and my heart is sick, help me release my deepest desires to You. Help me not to be self-reliant, but to respond to You in desperation. Help me trust You with my deepest desires. Enable me to understand that silence does not mean no. Empower me to fully release my deferred hopes to You.

▶ DECLARE

I trust in God's plan for me.

▶ ACT

Arrange a visit with a loved one in a desperate situation and pray with him or her.

56 God Multiplies Comfort

> Isaac brought her into the tent of his mother Sarah, and he married Rebekah. So she became his wife, and he loved her; and Isaac was comforted after his mother's death.
>
> Genesis 24:67 NIV

God promises to comfort you when your heart is breaking. This is a profound truth in itself, but the promise doesn't stop there. God also promises to comfort others through you!

When Isaac's mother died, God comforted him by uniting him with Rebekah. Isaac's comfort did not stop with him, though, but it spilled over into his wife's life as well. Rebekah had taken a huge step of faith when she married Isaac; she had gone to a place she didn't know to marry a man she had never met (see Genesis 24). In this sudden new reality, it must have been immensely comforting to learn that this stranger she had agreed to marry would *love* her.

God promises to multiply His comfort in your life as well. Paul says that God "comforts us in all our troubles, so that we can comfort those in any trouble with the comfort we ourselves receive from God" (2 Corinthians 1:4 NIV). As you reflect on how God has comforted you in your darkest times, consider how He might have you comfort those walking through similar trials.

God doesn't waste your grief, but He redeems it, comforting those in desperate need of hope through the hope He has given you.

▶ REFLECT

When have I experienced God's comfort?

▶ PRAY

Father God, I praise You for comforting me in my darkest times, and I thank You that You desire to comfort others through the comfort You have given me. Open my eyes to those experiencing grief today, and give me opportunities to speak into their lives with Your words of comfort and hope.

▶ DECLARE

God comforts others with the comfort He has given me.

▶ ACT

Reach out to someone in need of comfort today and encourage him or her, asking the Holy Spirit to guide your words and actions.

57 Abounding Hope

> Now may the God of hope fill you with all joy and peace in believing, that you may abound in hope by the power of the Holy Spirit.
>
> Romans 15:13 NKJV

Although some view the Bible merely as allegory, poetry, or an account of history past, it is the inspired, inerrant Word of the Living God. The words of Scripture are literally alive with God's miracle-working power and are able to penetrate the human soul and spirit (see Hebrews 4:12).

When the Bible speaks of God filling you with joy, it is not a figure of speech, but an actual event that occurs when you believe in His promises. God, by His Holy Spirit, dispenses both unexplainable joy and unshakable peace into every aspect of your mind, will and emotions.

To abound means "to have or possess in great quantity," such that despite the setting, the circumstances or your state of being, your confident hope wells up from within without measure. As you meditate on His Word, this knowledge of hope will grow from an intellectual concept to a tangible awareness of God's presence with you daily.

Anticipate the presence of the Holy Spirit in your life that continuously confirms the truthfulness of God's Word and His intention to bless you beyond anything you can think, ask or imagine (see Ephesians 3:20).

He is faithful to His Word, and He will keep His promises.

▶ REFLECT

How would your life change if you began to abound in joy, peace and hope?

▶ PRAY

Father God, I believe that You can cause me to abound in joy, peace, and hope by the power of Your Holy Spirit. I ask for renewed hope and the ability to see beyond the limitations of this natural realm, so I can align my faith with Your ability and see miracles abound.

▶ DECLARE

I abound in joy, peace and hope.

▶ ACT

Reach out to someone who needs hope, asking the Holy Spirit to use you as a conduit of His abounding hope.

58 Fully Restored

And the LORD restored the fortunes of Job, when he had prayed for his friends. And the LORD gave Job twice as much as he had before.

Job 42:10 ESV

God desires to restore you from past hurt, and forgiveness is often a part of that process. Although it is difficult to forgive, it is a powerful means through which God brings hope and restoration.

If anyone had a reason to deny forgiveness to others, it was Job. Through the loss of his children, health and livelihood, Job's friends did not support him but judged him. Despite how badly Job's friends had wounded him, God gave Job the responsibility of praying for them.

God tested Job's character through this process, and He tests our character in the same way. When we want to hold on to bitterness, He asks us to forgive those who have wronged us and take the initiative in reconciling with them. Praying for those who have wronged us demonstrates a heart submitted to the restoration process.

When Job prayed for his friends, God "restored his fortunes and gave him twice as much as he had before" (Job 42:10 NIV). Similarly, when we forgive, God replaces our bitterness with a joy that exceeds our expectations. Forgiveness may not change the other person, but it always changes us.

Embrace God's restorative process and wait in hope for His restoration.

▶ REFLECT

Whom do I need to forgive?

▶ PRAY

Father God, remind me that You are there when I am hurt. Thank You for Your restoration process. Help me to pray for and forgive those who have wronged me. Restore my heart as You restored Job's fortune. Thank You that this, too, will pass and work out for my good.

▶ DECLARE

God restores me as I pray for those who have wronged me.

▶ ACT

Take one step toward reconciliation with someone who has wronged you.

59 Hope for a Family Reunion

> But I do not want you to be ignorant, brethren, concerning those who have fallen asleep, lest you sorrow as others who have no hope. For if we believe that Jesus died and rose again, even so God will bring with Him those who sleep in Jesus.
>
> 1 Thessalonians 4:13–14 NKJV

Losing a loved one is one of the most painful of human experiences, but as a follower of Christ, you have hope that you will be reunited with your believing family members!

The story often recurs with similar heart-wrenching effect. A small child, too young to understand death, stands at a graveside, wondering if he will ever see his loved one again. Or a mother whose child precedes her in death wails at the funeral, "Why, God, why?"

In the short term, the "why" may seem to go unanswered, yet the apostle Paul is quite clear about the hope that we have. Unlike other philosophies, religions or spiritual perspectives, Christianity stands alone in providing its faithful followers with a clear articulation of what is to come beyond the grave.

More than focusing on cherub-faced angels on white puffy clouds, the entire New Testament speaks in detail about believers who have "gone to sleep in Christ" being present with Him and secure in His eternal care (2 Corinthians 5:5–8).

Our hope is forever set ablaze as we envision that great day when every believing loved one, as well as nations of believers who died since Jesus' resurrection, are all brought with God through Jesus into a glorious family reunion that never ends.

▶ REFLECT

Whom are you excited to be reunited with in heaven?

▶ PRAY

Father in heaven, when I grieve a believing loved one, fill me with the hope of our reunion in heaven. Thank You for giving us the gift of life with You in heaven. As I wait for the glorious reunion of believers, may I walk in a manner worthy of the hope to which You have called me.

▶ DECLARE

I will again see those who followed Jesus.

▶ ACT

Comfort someone who is grieving a believing loved one with a reminder of their future reunion in heaven.

60 Unfailing Mercy

> I recall this to my mind, therefore I wait. The LORD's acts of mercy indeed do not end, for His compassions do not fail. They are new every morning; great is Your faithfulness.
>
> Lamentations 3:21–23 NASB

Waiting for God to respond to your prayers can feel painful. Whether you are waiting for relief from affliction, for a fresh calling or for His promises to be delivered, there is a unique tension that occurs in waiting.

In this tension, it is easy to slip into doubt. *Did I really hear God? Did I do something to mess up God's plan? Am I stuck here forever? What should I do when my life feels like a rubber band stretched to the point of snapping?*

In this chapter of Lamentations, the prophet Jeremiah takes a deep breath. He stops recounting the ways he has been afflicted and instead recalls God's daily mercies in his life. As he recalls God's compassion, he is strengthened to wait on the future relief he knows is coming.

God's mercy does not stop. His fresh gifts of mercy appear *every single morning*. While we may look to the future with expectation and hope, we are actually experiencing God's goodness in the present. He is a faithful and compassionate Father who dwells with us in our waiting.

God knows what the future holds, and He is faithful to pour His mercy out on you with every sunrise.

▶ REFLECT

As I feel the tension of waiting for God to move in my situation, where do I currently see moments of His mercy in my life?

▶ PRAY

Lord, You always keep Your promises. You do not lie, and Your love for me is intimate and personal. I thank You for hearing my prayers and for the fresh portion of compassion and goodness You provide every day. Thank You for showing me love in big ways and small ones.

▶ DECLARE

God's mercies are new today.

▶ ACT

Think of a burden that you have been carrying that extends day after day. Declare repeatedly over this burden, "God's mercies are new today."

61 Scared, Yet Surrendered

And Deborah said to Barak, "Up! For this is the day in which the LORD has given Sisera into your hand. Does not the LORD go out before you?"

Judges 4:14 ESV

Has fear ever kept you from doing what God asked of you, although you had everything you needed?

Fear is such a powerful emotion that it can cripple obedience, keeping us from carrying out what God has empowered us to do. Fear produces unnecessary worry and regret, and it can even result in sickness. This is not God's plan for us!

God had commanded Barak to go to battle and equipped him with the tools he needed to be successful. Still, Barak was afraid. When Deborah reminded him that God's presence had gone ahead of him, though, he decided to obey despite his fear.

At times, God will ask us to do terrifying things, but we must set aside our fears and go anyway. Being afraid is never the problem; the problem is when fear keeps you from obeying God's instructions. We must decide whether fear or obedience will guide our steps.

When you obey God's instructions, you can trust that God's presence will go with you. God knows you are scared, and He will steady you as you carry out His will.

It is natural to be afraid, but obey the Lord anyway in the super-natural power of God.

▶ REFLECT

When was a time that fear gripped your heart, but God gave you the assurance that He was with you?

▶ PRAY

Father God, I release all of my fear to You. You have not given me the spirit of fear. You promise never to leave me nor forsake me. I thank You that I can do all things through Christ, who strengthens me. I surrender to Your plan, and I will obey.

▶ DECLARE

The Lord is the strength of my life; I am not afraid.

▶ ACT

Today, do one thing that you have been afraid to do.

62 Impossible Provision

> So she did as she was told. Her sons kept bringing jars to her, and she filled one after another. Soon every container was full to the brim!
>
> 2 Kings 4:5–6 NLT

Maintaining hope in dire need is difficult, just as living in lack is frustrating, scary and painful.

Often, when we are in need, we expect God to meet our needs our way. Instead, we should focus on God's provision more than on how He provides. In impossible situations, God often uses unlikely sources of provision.

The widow in 2 Kings experienced an unlikely source of provision. When her sons were to be taken as slaves by her late husband's creditor, the prophet Elisha instructed her to find as many containers as possible and fill them with her one jar of oil. God multiplied the oil, and she was able to sell it to save her sons from slavery.

Provision from God comes in a variety of ways. God uses His creativity and ingenuity to provide for us. He loves working things out for us in an original way. Although it is difficult to hope in impossible situations, God specializes in the impossible.

Invite God to do the impossible in your life. It is possible that you experience impossible situations because God wants you to see that He can do the impossible. God is your Provider, and He will provide for you.

▶ REFLECT

When has God proven Himself to be my Provider?

▶ PRAY

Father God, thank You for being my Provider. Thank You for all the times when You have provided in the past. Help me to remember Your faithfulness in provision. Remind me that You don't change and that You will provide for me both now and in the future. God, I thank You in advance for meeting all my needs.

▶ DECLARE

God always provides for me, even when it seems impossible.

▶ ACT

Today, be the hands and feet of Jesus, and find one person whom you can provide for today.

63 Fresh Life

> "I know that he will rise in the resurrection on the last day." Jesus said to her, "I am the resurrection and the life; the one who believes in Me will live, even if he dies."

John 11:24–25 NASB

Is there anything that feels more final than death? Whether it's the death of someone you love, or the death of a dream, death feels like the end. Even for believers, the sting of death still hurts.

Martha's statement to Jesus is powerful because she had no reason to believe her brother, Lazarus, would rise from the dead. Her only hope was that they would meet again in eternity. Jesus' response is even more powerful as He proclaims that death actually does not have finality, but that He offers eternal life.

The fact that Jesus is the resurrection and the life gives us hope. Even if we do lose precious things and people, new life is promised to those who believe. You may see restoration in this life, but regardless of whether or not you experience earthly restoration, you are promised life and restoration on the other side of death.

If you have lost something precious to death or defeat, even if it was years ago, ask the Lord to comfort your heart and to replace the sting of death with the hope of fresh life.

You can have hope that with Him, death will never have the final word.

▶ REFLECT

In what area have I experienced a "death" and am I believing for resurrection life?

▶ PRAY

Lord, I thank You for being the solution to death. You stole its finality when You died and rose again. Thank You for the promise of life and the hope of resurrection. I ask that You comfort my heart today and pour fresh life into the areas I have considered dead.

▶ DECLARE

Jesus brings life to what was once dead.

▶ ACT

Identify an area of your life that you have considered dead. Talk to someone about how you would like to see that area redeemed and ask him or her to pray with you.

64 Hope in the Promise Keeper

"And I will bring you to the land I swore with uplifted hand to give to Abraham, to Isaac and to Jacob. I will give it to you as a possession. I am the LORD."

Exodus 6:8 NIV

Have you ever found yourself in a situation so discouraging that you failed to believe God's promises and instead believed that He had forgotten you?

The Israelites did just this. After the Lord declared that they would enter the Promised Land, Israel did not listen "because of their discouragement and harsh labor" (verse 9). They had lost hope and felt abandoned by God.

God reminded the Israelites He had not forgotten them and would be with them, pointing to the promise He had made to their fathers, Abraham, Isaac and Jacob, that a great inheritance awaited them. He reminded Israel of this promise while they were still in captivity, and He reminds you today that there is hope for your deliverance. In the middle of your struggle, remember that God always keeps His promises.

Psalm 30:5 (NKJV) says, "Weeping may endure for a night, but joy comes in the morning." Like the Israelites, you may feel discouraged by your current circumstances, but you can be confident that God has not forgotten you and is working all things for your good.

God is your Promise Keeper, and He will fulfill His Word.

▶ REFLECT

What promise from God am I holding on to?

▶ PRAY

Father, renew my faith in Your promises. Help me to keep my eyes on what You have said, not what I see or don't see. You are a Promise Keeper and will do the things You said You will do in my life. I trust You, and I thank You that You are working all things together for my good!

▶ DECLARE

God is a Promise Keeper.

▶ ACT

Write down a promise God has made (including Scriptures) that has not yet come to pass. Place it somewhere visible, and every time you see it, thank Him for what He will do.

65 A Way in the Wilderness

"Behold, I am doing a new thing; now it springs forth, do you not perceive it? I will make a way in the wilderness and rivers in the desert."

Isaiah 43:19 ESV

Life's challenges can make it difficult to discern God's goodness, but you can trust that God is always doing a new thing in your life.

God wants us to look closely at what He is doing, but this can be easy to miss when we are overwhelmed. There will be times when we will miss the blessing of family time because we are at home unemployed from a job that previously kept us away from our families. We can overlook the blessing of companionship during an illness when we previously suffered from painstaking loneliness. We often do not perceive the obvious blessings of God because we are preoccupied with the negativity in our lives.

When this happens, the Holy Spirit will direct our eyes to focus on the new things God is doing. God is excited to bring new things into our lives and make pathways where we have yet to travel. He takes pleasure in creating rivers of living waters in the driest places.

Look for the new things that God is doing in your life amid your challenges. Know that God is walking with you, and hope in the new things God wants to do in you, for you and through you.

▶ REFLECT

In what area do you perceive God doing something new?

▶ PRAY

Father God, thank You for focusing my attention on You. Thank You for the newness that You bring in the midst of daily challenges. Help me to put my hope in Your goodness, especially when things are not good. Thank You for making ways when there are none. Thank You for bringing new water into the dry places in my life.

▶ DECLARE

God is doing something new in my life.

▶ ACT

Step out in faith by taking a small risk in the area where you believe God is doing something new in your life.

66 A Different Spirit

> But because my servant Caleb has a different spirit and follows me wholeheartedly, I will bring him into the land he went to, and his descendants will inherit it.
>
> Numbers 14:24 NIV

When God calls you to step out in faith, others may try to discourage you, saying that what He has asked of you simply cannot be done. You can defy their voices, for God always equips those He calls.

When the twelve spies returned from scouting out the Promised Land, the majority allowed fear to control them and argued against entering the land to which God had called them. Caleb, however, stood up against the majority, confident that since God had promised victory, He would grant victory. God rewarded Caleb's faith, not only allowing him to be one of only two people in his generation to enter the Promised Land, but blessing him with the legacy of a "different spirit."

If you confess Jesus Christ as Lord, you, too, have a different Spirit! Romans 8:9 says that "you are controlled by the Spirit if you have the Spirit of God living in you" (NLT). The Holy Spirit is working to comfort, convict and empower you to fulfill your purpose on earth.

Just like Caleb, act in courageous hope, confident that God will equip you for the work He has called you to do.

▶ **REFLECT**

In what area is God calling me to act confidently and boldly?

▶ **PRAY**

Father God, thank You for empowering me to act courageously through the power of the Holy Spirit. When others discourage me from following You, remind me that You are trustworthy. When fear paralyzes me, remind me that You equip those You call. Make me like Caleb so that I may boldly walk out your purpose for me.

▶ **DECLARE**

The Holy Spirit leads me, and I follow Him.

▶ **ACT**

Choose one way to act confidently and boldly this day as a follower of Christ, asking the Holy Spirit to empower you with courage.

67

Hope for Immortality

"In the beginning, Lord, you laid the foundation of the earth and made the heavens with your hands. They will perish, but you remain forever. They will wear out like old clothing. You will fold them up like a cloak and discard them like old clothing. But you are always the same; you will live forever."

Hebrews 1:10–12 NLT

Right now, you are bound by time, but one day, it will hold no power over you.

When we are born into this world, we begin the journey of earthly life that, at its longest, will last 120 years. Yet here, the writer of Hebrews speaks of Jesus as One who not only began outside the construct of time, but who supersedes it—remaining eternally unchanged by its effects.

We, too, will one day stand perfected, incorruptible and impervious to time, for when we see Jesus, we shall be like Him (see 1 John 3:2). He will render aging and sickness powerless, and death will be a distant memory. By the power of His blood, our lives will not be extinguished after a century, but they will continue for all eternity.

We are even referred to as citizens of the new city of Jerusalem, which is portrayed as both a spiritual and physical place that descends from the heavenly realms to hover within visual range of the natural Jerusalem now below (see Revelation 21:2).

This is why Jesus lived and died: for you to have the opportunity to experience eternity as a beloved citizen of heaven and a member of His divine family.

▶ REFLECT

How does my hope of eternity with Christ affect how I live my life?

▶ PRAY

Jesus, help me understand more about eternity with You. In the midst of this mortal world, may I not be discouraged by the effects of time, but may I take heart as I remember that one day, time will hold no power over me. Help me to live today with this eternal perspective.

▶ DECLARE

I will live with Christ for eternity.

▶ ACT

Search the internet for "world history timeline." Review the last three thousand years of recorded history, then reflect on the fact that eternity will last longer than the longest timeline recorded on earth multiplied many times over.

68

God's Merciful Heart

> When God saw their deeds, that they turned from their evil way,
> then God relented of the disaster which He had declared He would
> bring on them. So He did not do it.
>
> Jonah 3:10 NASB

When you repent of your sin and ask for God's forgiveness, do you believe He wants to forgive you and cancel His judgment? Do you think He delights in mercy, or is He eager to dole out punishment?

Nineveh was a city with a death sentence. They were completely absorbed in their sin, and God couldn't withhold His judgment any longer. He commissioned Jonah to go to Nineveh and give the people one last chance to turn from their wickedness. Despite his rather famous detour, Jonah eventually obeyed and delivered God's message: The city had forty days to repent, or God would destroy it.

God gave the people of Nineveh a way out, and the entire city repented of their sin. He canceled His judgment because He deeply longs to forgive. If God delighted in punishment, He would never have sent Jesus, but He gave everything He had to ensure that we had a way out of judgment.

His heart toward you is tender, and He desires to forgive you. He wants to be close to you, and you can have hope that no one wants to extend mercy more than He does. He is just waiting for you to ask.

▶ REFLECT

What have I done that I wonder if God is willing to forgive?

▶ PRAY

Lord, thank You for desiring closeness and intimacy with me. Thank You for giving me every opportunity to be redeemed back unto You. I want to be made completely right with You, and I believe that You want to forgive my sins. Thank You for Your mercy and Your abundant love.

▶ DECLARE

God willingly forgives me.

▶ ACT

Sit with the Lord and let Him search your heart. If He highlights a sin, confess it, knowing He delights in forgiving you.

69 Relentless Hope

> Then she lived as a widow to the age of eighty-four. She never left the Temple but stayed there day and night, worshiping God with fasting and prayer.
>
> Luke 2:37 NLT

God always fulfills His promises, but when the wait is long, it can be easy to doubt this truth. In the waiting, you can cultivate a relentless hope in Him through a lifestyle of worship, prayer and fasting.

Have you ever known anyone who hoped in God like Anna did? Anna prayed, fasted and waited day and night for a prophetic word of the Messiah to be fulfilled. This relentless woman intended to see God's promise fulfilled, and she did.

Anna's consistent prayer and fasting demonstrated a relentless hope in God. Relentless hope in God eases the pain of waiting, as your attention is heaven-centered and your heart is postured in faith. Continual worship, prayer and fasting build spiritual muscles, which ignite the hope and faith that ultimately produce fulfilled promises.

Suppose you adopted a lifestyle like this where you need to see a promise fulfilled? Since God fulfills every promise He ever makes, you can posture your heart in hope and build your faith.

Demonstrating your relentless hope in God will ensure that you are unashamed at His coming.

God is waiting for your relentless hope, and He will be faithful to respond to it.

▶ **REFLECT**

When has something I eagerly hoped for come to pass?

▶ **PRAY**

Father God, help me to be relentless in my worshiping, praying and fasting. Help me to focus on what You have already promised so that I may receive the promises of God in my life. Help me to trust that You hear my prayers, that You recognize my sacrifices in fasting and that You will reward me with fulfilled promises.

▶ **DECLARE**

My hope is relentless because God is always faithful.

▶ **ACT**

In a step toward relentless hope, fast from a meal today (if your health allows) and spend that time in prayer.

70

God Proves Himself

> At the usual time for offering the evening sacrifice, Elijah the prophet walked up to the altar and prayed, "O LORD, God of Abraham, Isaac, and Jacob, prove today that you are God in Israel and that I am your servant. Prove that I have done all this at your command."
>
> 1 Kings 18:36 NLT

Has your hope ever been challenged because you saw no way out? It is hard to hope when you feel trapped by a lack of solutions, but God is worthy of your hope, even in situations that seem hopeless.

When Elijah asked God to prove Himself before the prophets of Baal by sending fire for a burnt offering, the situation was hopeless in human terms. Elijah had so much hope in God's ability to ignite the sacrifice, though, that he doused the altar with water. His hope in God was not disappointed (see 1 Kings 18:20–39).

When we face situations that appear impossible, we must also posture our hearts in hope. Like God did in Elijah's life, when there is nothing left to do but hope in God, this is the time when God shows up as a Way Maker. We often miss divine encounters with God because we lose hope and give up right before He shows up.

We have to train ourselves not to focus on the situation, but on God. God can be trusted.

God will meet you where you are when you hope in Him. When you can do nothing else, God can do miracles.

▶ REFLECT

What is God saying about a seemingly impossible situation in your life?

▶ PRAY

Father God, as I face hopeless situations, help me to remember that You are with me. Help me remember always to approach You for solutions, even if there appear to be none. Teach me to trust You completely. Show me Your glory, and show me how to discern Your leading as I seek solutions.

▶ DECLARE

God does miracles on my behalf.

▶ ACT

Call a friend who is in a seemingly hopeless situation and encourage him or her with Scriptures and personal stories of how God has worked in hopeless circumstances.

71

Hope amid Persecution

> But he, being full of the Holy Spirit, gazed into heaven and saw the glory of God, and Jesus standing at the right hand of God, and said, "Look! I see the heavens opened and the Son of Man standing at the right hand of God!"
>
> Acts 7:55–56 NKJV

Stephen the martyr's final words both thrill and challenge believers today.

Despite facing certain death, he was emboldened to testify of the truth of Jesus' resurrection and subsequent ministry at the right hand of God the Father. He did not attempt to placate the surrounding mob, which was rabid in its desire to cast the first stone. His singular focus was to deliver truth and bring honor to Jesus.

In response to his faith and willingness to stand up for the truth of the Gospel, something amazing happened. When Stephen gazed into heaven, he saw Jesus standing at God's right hand. History illustrates the fact that kings only stand when someone deserving great honor or acknowledgment is brought into their presence. Jesus was, in effect, standing to greet Stephen as he was stoned by the surrounding mob.

This is how Jesus responds to those who suffer persecution. He is not merely aware of their situation, but He empowers them to withstand the onslaught until the end and ultimately welcomes them into His eternal presence.

If you face persecution, focus on the image of Jesus standing at God's right hand, looking on your faithfulness with joy and empowering you to stand firm to the end.

▶ **REFLECT**

How have I responded to persecution in the past?

▶ **PRAY**

Jesus, thank You for welcoming Stephen into Your presence as he boldly shared the Good News with his killers. Give me the boldness of Stephen in whatever type of persecution I face, be it verbal, relational or physical, knowing that You are pleased by even the smallest act of faithfulness.

▶ **DECLARE**

God gives me boldness in the face of persecution.

▶ **ACT**

Search the internet for "persecuted Christians" and find an organization that supports persecuted followers of Jesus. Pray for the country or situation that the Holy Spirit lays on your heart.

72 | God Goes before Me

> "Do not be afraid or discouraged, for the LORD will personally go ahead of you. He will be with you; he will neither fail you nor abandon you."
>
> Deuteronomy 31:8 NLT

When you take a road trip, it is important to have a map or GPS to guide you to your destination. The Holy Spirit is like a trusty map, giving you perfect directions on your "road trip" of life.

The Holy Spirit goes before you to pave your way. Psalm 37:23 says, "The LORD makes firm the steps of the one who delights in him" (NIV). Although you cannot anticipate all the obstacles you will encounter, He is aware of them and already knows how He will guide you when you face them.

Scripture says that the Holy Spirit will lead you into all truth, counsel you and comfort you. When you come to a fork in the road and are not sure which way to turn, the Holy Spirit will show you the way. When you get tired and want to quit, He will refresh you. When you are afraid of moving into uncharted territory, He will give you courage.

You can take your next steps with faith, steadiness and hope. He has promised to guide and strengthen you as you follow Him.

► **REFLECT**

When have I experienced the Holy Spirit's guidance on my life's journey?

► **PRAY**

Lord, I am so grateful that You accompany me on my life's journey. When the road is dark, You light the way. When there are roadblocks, You go before me to clear them. When I am lost, You set me on the proper course. Help me to remember that I can have hope in Your promise to guide me.

► **DECLARE**

The Holy Spirit guides me.

► **ACT**

Perceive the Holy Spirit's presence with you today. Listen to His directions and follow His guidance.

73 Reconciliation with God

"I will betroth you to Me forever; yes, I will betroth you to Me in righteousness and justice, in lovingkindness and mercy."

Hosea 2:19 NKJV

When you sin, your first instinct may be to hide from God, thinking He wants nothing to do with you. But God wants you to remember He has betrothed you to Himself in an eternal covenant of love!

The book of Hosea shows the lengths to which God went to indicate His intentions toward His people, Israel. God told the righteous prophet Hosea to seek out and marry a prostitute. God called Hosea to do this to illustrate how the people of Israel had committed spiritual adultery against Him by worshiping pagan idols. These pagan practices had horrific effects on the lives of His people, Israel, and especially upon the lives of their children.

Despite God's people actively participating in what God considered an abomination multiple times throughout their history, God utters the prophetic promise that He will make a way to ultimately erase Israel's sin. He promises to make a forever covenant with her, which He fulfilled in the death and resurrection of Jesus (see Matthew 26:28).

No matter how far you have fallen, God is *ever willing* to reconcile with you when you seek forgiveness and pursue true repentance.

▶ REFLECT

How would I act if I knew everything between God and me was good?

▶ PRAY

Holy Spirit, reveal anything separating me from perfect fellowship with God, my Father. Lead me through the steps of repentance, reminding me that I may boldly approach the throne of grace. Show me what You consider to be spiritual adultery, so I am watchful to keep my heart pure and faithful toward You.

▶ DECLARE

I am reconciled to God through the blood of Jesus.

▶ ACT

Take care of anything separating you from God. Then celebrate in some way your relationship with Him, knowing you are reconciled completely to Him.

74 A Righteous Legacy

> And he did what was right in the sight of the LORD . . . ; he did not turn aside to the right hand or to the left.
>
> 2 Kings 22:2 NKJV

How do you want to be remembered? As a follower of Christ, how wonderful would it be for your memory to be defined by doing what was right in God's sight!

Yet as you read the account of King Josiah's lifelong righteousness, you may wonder if it is possible for *you*.

Fear not! There is hope for those of us who live in today's world and who desire to live a life of commitment to God and His ways. Although God enabled Josiah to live righteously within the structure of the Old Covenant, Josiah did not have the benefit of being constantly indwelt by the Holy Spirit as we are.

What a privilege we have—unfettered access to the Holy Spirit, whose purpose is to guide us into all truth, and to Jesus at the throne of Almighty God, making continuous intercession for us until He returns as King. We truly have all we need for life and godliness (see 2 Peter 1:3).

He is both willing and able to keep you from falling. Walk forward in confidence that through His power, you can leave behind a legacy of righteousness that illuminates His glory.

▶ REFLECT

How do you want to be remembered?

▶ PRAY

Holy Spirit, fill me daily with the desire and the ability to keep the commitments I have made to You. You know what I will face today, tomorrow and every day until I meet You face-to-face. Open my eyes to Your ability so that I, too, can walk worthy of Your high calling.

▶ DECLARE

The Holy Spirit empowers me to do what is right.

▶ ACT

Today, be aware of the legacy you want to leave and be deliberate to do what is right in God's sight.

75 Unashamed Hope

> When he heard that it was Jesus of Nazareth, he began to shout, "Jesus, Son of David, have mercy on me!" Many rebuked him and told him to be quiet, but he shouted all the more, "Son of David, have mercy on me!"
>
> Mark 10:47–48 NIV

When the Holy Spirit wants you to speak, you may be tempted to silence yourself, fearing what others may think. If you are afraid, remember that God's favor is far sweeter than human praise.

When the blind man Bartimaeus cried out to Jesus for healing, many tried to silence him. Perhaps they were embarrassed at the scene he was making or jealous of his bold request. Bartimaeus could have stopped crying out to preserve his dignity, but he refused to keep quiet. Since he was fully convinced of Jesus' goodness and power, human approval meant nothing to him. Although the crowd rebuked him, Jesus *called* him and honored his faith with healing.

In a world that views faith as childish and unsophisticated, it is not easy to speak about Jesus to those around us. Remembering the example of Bartimaeus, do not quiet yourself, but refuse to be swayed by human criticism. Speak boldly, anchored by hope in the God who not only healed the blind, but has given you the gift of eternal life!

Jesus has invited you to speak His words of hope to the lost, and He will empower you to do it.

▶ REFLECT

To whom does God desire that I speak the truth more boldly?

▶ PRAY

Father God, I confess that at times, I have not spoken about You because I have feared others' opinions. Impress upon me just how much more valuable Your praise is than the praise of humans. Holy Spirit, make me sensitive to Your leadings, embolden me and use me as Your ambassador today!

▶ DECLARE

God empowers me to speak boldly for Him.

▶ ACT

Ask the Holy Spirit to bring a person to mind, and then share with him or her boldly whatever the Holy Spirit leads you to say.

76 Hope Anchors Us

> This hope we have as an anchor of the soul, a hope both sure and reliable and one which enters within the veil.
>
> Hebrews 6:19 NASB

God's promises bring hope. But when you read these promises, what negative or doubtful thoughts bubble up around them? Do you find yourself wondering if such promises are too good to be true?

Boats that are anchored will remain in place even in the wildest storms. They may strain against the ropes, and sometimes the connecting rope may even break as the boat pulls against it, but the anchor never moves.

If you have suffered betrayal or disappointment, it can be easy to question whether God can be trusted. We can take God at His Word because it is impossible for Him to lie. Lying is a sin, and He is without sin, so it is impossible for Him to lie, exaggerate or fall short of His promise. We may choose to give up or walk away, but He cannot. He will do what He said He would do.

The next time doubt seeps in, remember that God's promises to you cannot be broken. Even in terrible storms or in the subtle rumblings of your own doubts, He is a safe and secure anchor.

▶ REFLECT

What thoughts or emotions do I have that need to be anchored in hope?

▶ PRAY

Father, attend to my fears, anxiety, cynicism and doubt. You know where it springs from, and I invite You in to heal those memories and give me hope again. Help me to believe in every word You say and remember that You cannot lie or fall short. I place my hope in You alone, for You are my safe and secure anchor.

▶ DECLARE

God's hope is reliable and anchors my soul.

▶ ACT

Talk to God about any thoughts or emotions that need to be anchored in hope. Repeat the prayer and declaration above as often as needed.

77 Fear No Man

> The LORD is my light and my salvation; whom should I fear? The
> LORD is the defense of my life; whom should I dread?
>
> Psalm 27:1 NASB

Who has power over your well-being and future? Is it your boss?
Is it a parent, a spouse, a child or a governmental authority? Do
you ever feel frightened or threatened by those in power over
your life?

While we are called to respect those in power over us, we are
never told to fear them. In fact, the only person we are repeatedly
told to fear is God. He is the One who protects and provides for
us. He is the defense of our life and a safe place for our heart. He
has the power to cast angels into hell and the compassion to hold
us like a Father when we are in our deepest suffering.

When fear of man starts to bubble up inside of us, we are called
to remember that all power and authority come from God. We
have nothing to fear if we are pursuing the Lord and His will for our
life. It is only when we step outside of His will that we put ourselves
in dangerous positions.

His heart toward you is good, and you can rest in the hope
that man can do nothing to separate you from the love of God.

► REFLECT

Whom or what do I fear?

► PRAY

Father, You did not create me to fear man. I pray that You would fill my mind and heart with holy peace and teach me what it means to have a righteous fear and reverence of You alone. Where I feel threatened, bring me a clear understanding of who holds power over my life.

► DECLARE

I will not fear, for God is with me.

► ACT

Jot down the name of one person who has power over your life and ask God to help you see that person as He sees them.

78 Hope in the Living God

> For to this end we toil and strive, because we have our hope set on the living God, who is the Savior of all people, especially of those who believe.
>
> 1 Timothy 4:10 ESV

There is something immensely powerful about setting your hope upon something. When you set your hope on something and are committed to realizing the thing hoped for, not only is the target in question seen as a future possibility, but it also becomes a source of faith and anticipation.

The apostle Paul had set his hope on the living God, and his hope became the psychological and physical fuel needed to accomplish the labor of traveling the known world. It also spurred him to write the majority of the New Testament to spread the Good News and lay Christianity's earliest foundations. This hope led him into and through situations and circumstances that required much labor and required suffering life-threatening reproach.

Why did Paul persist? The answer: He knew he was serving the Source of salvation for all humanity. The confidence Paul had in God strengthened him in his weakness and helped him to endure persecution.

As a follower of Christ, the hope you have in Him will strengthen and steady you in your suffering. When you fix your eyes on your eternal hope, your spiritual eyes will be opened, and persecution will seem inconsequential in comparison to your glorious future.

▶ REFLECT

What persecution or suffering can I put in perspective by fixing my eyes on the living God?

▶ PRAY

God of salvation, by the power of Your Holy Spirit, refocus our hope upon You both now and in the eternal future to come. Give me clarity as to how I should labor and strive toward the things You have called me to do. May I follow You daily, emulating Jesus, following Your directives.

▶ DECLARE

My hope is in the living God.

▶ ACT

Tell someone you trust about an area of suffering or persecution you are experiencing. Pray together and declare your hope in God.

79 Hope That Doesn't Disappoint

And hope does not disappoint, because the love of God has been poured out within our hearts through the Holy Spirit who was given to us.

Romans 5:5 NASB

What moments in your life have been disappointing? Have you ever felt a spark of hope ignite like a freshly lit candle, only to watch it flicker and die when "life happened"? Has that changed how you approach life?

If your heart or your hope has been disappointed, letting new hope in can feel like a betrayal of your own trust. As humans, we learn from experience, so disappointment can teach us that people, situations or even God cannot be trusted because the fallout from disappointment is so painful. But what does God say about hope?

In Romans 5, Paul is speaking about disappointment and hardships. He states that there is fruit in tribulations when the ultimate goal is the glory of God. If our hope is placed in our own glory or in the things of this world, it will disappoint, but when we focus on glorifying God, even our greatest losses reap brilliant rewards.

Disappointments still sting, losses are real and it takes true faith and courage to let hope be reignited in your heart. But if your heart is set on the Father, you can trust that He will not let your hope be snuffed out.

▶ REFLECT

When have I experienced the greatest disappointment?

▶ PRAY

Father, forgive me for placing hope in the futile and fleeting things of this world. I choose today to place my hope in You and Your glory, neither of which can disappoint. You are who You say You are, and You will fulfill all You have promised. Thank You for being a safe place for me to invest my hope.

▶ DECLARE

My hope is set on God, who will not disappoint me.

▶ ACT

Remember a time when you were disappointed. Ask the Holy Spirit to show you how He was with you in that time, then thank Him for His presence in that moment.

80 Hope for New Life

> And Adam knew his wife again, and she bore a son and called his name Seth, for she said, "God has appointed for me another offspring instead of Abel, for Cain killed him."
>
> Genesis 4:25 ESV

Not only does God know the pain and hurt of every loss, but He is with you to guide you into new life!

Death or loss can leave us in new, unexpected places. After Cain murdered Abel, Eve found herself in a state of intense grief that she had never experienced before. Yet, even in the midst of this overwhelming, unexpected grief, she was not without hope because she knew God was there. When Eve bore another son, she recognized it was God's hand that had provided this new life.

Although you may know God is with you in your pain, grief, anxiety, fear and hopelessness can still be paralyzing. To embrace the new life God has for you, you must grapple with the pain and accept the reality of the loss. Your response to your loss and to God in this unexpected, new place is vital.

Negative responses can lead to anger, resentment and depression, which yield the fruit of darkness. Positive responses lead us into acceptance, submission and surrender, which produce new, unexpected worship.

God never wastes His children's pain. As Eve experienced new life with the birth of Seth, God will bring unexpected beauty from your unexpected loss.

▶ REFLECT

In what area have I experienced death where I am hoping for new life?

▶ PRAY

Father God, help me process the pain of this death or loss. Help me accept this newness and embrace Your abiding presence. Lord, increase my trust and faith. God, You can bring life from this death. I desire Your glory even in this, and I ask that one day, I may help others who are navigating a new reality as well.

▶ DECLARE

God gives beauty for ashes.

▶ ACT

Reach out to encourage someone who has experienced an unexpected loss.

81 God Rescues

"My God sent His angel and shut the lions' mouths, and they have not harmed me, since I was found innocent before Him; and also toward you, O king, I have committed no crime."

Daniel 6:22 NASB

What feels hopeless to you today? What are you facing that feels like a lost cause? Do you feel like the decision has been made and everything is beyond hope?

Daniel knew about hopeless situations. His people had been enslaved by an enemy king. That same king restricted the religious freedoms of the Israelites, and because of Daniel's obedience to God, the king sentenced Daniel to death. Imagine what was going through Daniel's mind as he hit the hard floor of the pit and saw the lions start to stir. Most of us would have despaired.

However, Daniel knew that he had been obedient to God. He had been faithful, and God does not forget the faithfulness of His children. He does not always rescue us in the way we hope, but even if our obedience leads to our earthly death, we have been rescued by Jesus' sacrifice on the cross. With God, we have hope that He will redeem and rescue our situation.

As you assess the parts of your life that feel beyond rescue, trust that God is both able and willing to rescue you. Converse with your Father and ask Him boldly as His child to move in your situation.

▶ **REFLECT**

Where do I need God to rescue me?

▶ **PRAY**

Lord, You are my Father, and You have already rescued my soul for eternity. I am so grateful for all You have done. As I face situations that feel hopeless or when I am overwhelmed by fear, I ask that You would rescue and redeem all that I thought was lost.

▶ **DECLARE**

God is my rescuer.

▶ **ACT**

Reach out to someone who has come through the other side of a difficulty you are currently facing. Ask him or her to share insights and pray with you.

Hope for the Unseen

So because our hope is set on what is yet to be seen, we patiently keep on waiting for its fulfillment.

Romans 8:25 TPT

What is something you are hoping for? How long have you been waiting? As you wait on what you are hoping for, what doubts have crept in?

John the Baptist lived a radical life. He and Jesus were born around the same time, so John was about thirty years old when he baptized Jesus. We do not know how long he wandered in the wilderness preparing Jesus' path, but it could have been many years.

There must have been moments when he questioned his decision to leave home, dress in animal skins and live on locusts and wild honey in the wilderness. There must have been days of doubt and a desire for a normal, comfortable life, but John was faithful to complete his task. When Jesus did arrive at the Jordan River, every doubt and moment of wondering was redeemed.

It's okay to feel discouraged in the waiting. It's okay to question; God will not be offended. Today, praise Him for always keeping His Word, and do the most recent thing He told you to do with faithfulness. Trust that His timing is perfect.

▶ REFLECT

What hope have I abandoned because I've had to wait for a long time?

▶ PRAY

Jesus, I'm frustrated that I have had to wait so long, but I choose to trust You. Forgive me for the times I have tried to force Your hand to move faster, or when I have abandoned hope because the wait felt too long. Restore my hope, and help me to keep on waiting patiently on Your exquisite timing for its fulfillment.

▶ DECLARE

God's timing is perfect.

▶ ACT

Turn your waiting into thanksgiving. Recall the many times when God has fulfilled your hopes and thank Him.

83 Remember God's Faithfulness

The LORD your God has blessed you in all the work of your hands. He has watched over your journey through this vast wilderness. These forty years the LORD your God has been with you, and you have not lacked anything.

Deuteronomy 2:7 NIV

Whether you are struggling to make a decision or facing an unexpected trial, it is easy to be overwhelmed by fear. Reflecting on God's faithfulness in the past is a powerful way to give you hope for the future!

While the Israelites wandered in the desert after God had freed them from slavery, He not only provided for them and kept them safe, but He *blessed* them. Still, God's people needed to be reminded of what He had done if they were to face the future without fear. When experiencing new and daunting trials, we tend to forget how God has provided for us every step of the way, seeing only the immensity of the problem before us.

But God desires to free you of any shortsightedness by reminding you of the vivid history of His faithfulness in your life. If you ask Him, He will joyfully lead you through the story of your life and remind you of the times when He comforted you in grief, gave you wisdom, provided for you and blessed you.

No matter how insurmountable your problems seem today, you can step forward with confident hope, steadied and strengthened by the remembrance of His faithfulness.

▶ REFLECT

How has God shown His faithfulness in my life?

▶ PRAY

Father God, as I face the problems and questions of today, I confess any fearfulness or anxiety that is controlling my mind. Remind me of specific times when You have provided for me, given me wisdom and acted on my behalf, and fill me with clear-eyed hope as I walk into the future.

▶ DECLARE

God is always faithful to me.

▶ ACT

Share a story of God's faithfulness in your life with a friend or family member.

Hope Brings Endurance

> Constantly keeping in mind your work of faith and labor of love and perseverance of hope in our Lord Jesus Christ in the presence of our God and Father.
>
> 1 Thessalonians 1:3 NASB

If you have ever had a coach, you may have heard the phrase "When things get tough, remember your *why*."

In this passage, Paul praises the church's "work of faith," "labor of love" and "perseverance of hope in our Lord Jesus Christ" because he knows how easy it is to be blown off course by trials and pain. As the church was growing and experiencing challenges and persecution, their "why" was Jesus. They wanted His glory and the hope that comes from following Him. They had a long and hard road ahead of them, but fixing their hope on Christ gave them endurance.

Living a life that is surrendered to God can be challenging. He never promises that obedience will feel good, but we are promised so much on the other side of our obedience. When embedded in our hearts, hope can spur us on through tremendous difficulties.

As you experience challenges, remember where your hope lies. Putting your hope in Christ gives you the fortitude to endure any trial that comes your way. Putting your hope in Christ both comforts you and propels you forward.

When your "why" is the hope you have in Christ, you will be able to run the race with endurance.

▶ REFLECT

Where am I needing fresh endurance today?

▶ PRAY

Father, You know better than anyone what trials and hardships I face. You know my innermost desires and thoughts. Help me to set You as the goal of my pursuit and the ultimate joy of my life so that when things get tough, my hope in You will give me endurance unto victory.

▶ DECLARE

I can endure all things when Jesus is my goal.

▶ ACT

Consider an area where you need endurance. Ask a fellow believer to pray for your strength and that your focus would be on the hope you have in Christ.

85 Hope in God's Power

"It is true, LORD, that the Assyrian kings have laid waste these nations and their lands. . . . Now, LORD our God, deliver us from his hand, so that all the kingdoms of the earth may know that you alone, LORD, are God."

2 Kings 19:17, 19 NIV

Are you facing something that seems insurmountable? Human understanding and logic may tell you that triumph is not possible, but the truth is that you have hope for victory because you serve the God of the *impossible*.

King Hezekiah also faced a humanly impossible trial. King Sennacherib, of Assyria, demanded that he surrender, his field commander gloating that Hezekiah was outnumbered and that Assyria had demolished other nations with ease. Hezekiah, though, refused to let Sennacherib's taunts influence him (see 2 Kings 18–19). Instead of letting the enemy's words besiege his mind, he fixed his thoughts on the one true God and trusted in His power. God honored Hezekiah's trust and delivered His people from the mighty nation of Assyria.

When the enemy's taunts assault your mind, remember that you serve the same God as Hezekiah did, whose work is not constrained by human limits and whose power makes man's pale in comparison.

Even in the most impossible of circumstances, you can walk forward in a solid hope that does not trust in the lies of the enemy, but in the words of the all-powerful God. He cherishes your trust, and He will act on your behalf.

▶ REFLECT

In what area do I need to ignore the voice of my enemies and trust in God's voice instead?

▶ PRAY

Father God, the enemy has taunted me with the lie that You cannot or will not help me overcome the trial I am facing. Like Hezekiah, I refuse to let these lies influence my thoughts and actions. I trust in You, Almighty God, to steady me with hope, show me Your power and lead me to victory.

▶ DECLARE

God is infinitely more powerful than my enemies.

▶ ACT

With your eyes fixed on God's power, do something you have been putting off because you have been listening to the lies of the enemy.

86 Resurrected Life

"I will put flesh and muscles on you and cover you with skin. I will put breath into you, and you will come to life. Then you will know that I am the LORD."

Ezekiel 37:6 NLT

Extended times of waiting, suffering and trials can cause our hope, faith and trust to dry up and even die. God wants to resurrect your hope and your life!

When our hope dies, our hearts become sick, and we find ourselves feeling despondent. In our despair, darkness tries to rob us of everything. Yet God gave us the ability to live an abundant life. We often think of resurrection as only applicable to the raising of the dead, but it is applicable to our hope as well. God wants to use you and your life as a testament that the resurrection of hope is possible.

God showed His resurrection power when He told Ezekiel to prophesy life to dead bones. These dead bones represented Israel in its despair, whose "bones [were] dried up and . . . hope [was] gone" (Ezekiel 37:11 NIV). God miraculously put flesh on the bones and breathed His life into them, a sure sign that the Lord lives and that He is faithful to resurrect the hope of His people.

God has given you the power of life in your tongue. You can speak God's promises to your dead hope and command it to live. He wants you to see the power of resurrection in your hope, in your circumstances and in your life.

▶ REFLECT

Where do I need my hope to be resurrected?

▶ PRAY

Father God, I need a fresh wind of faith and fire. Renew my hope and confidence in Your Word. Give me grace to wait on You, and increase my strength as I wait. Help me not to grow weary. Spirit of God, put Your breath into me and bring me back to life. As You resurrected the dry bones, resurrect my hope in Your promises.

▶ DECLARE

God breathes His life into me.

▶ ACT

Be honest with someone about hope that has died in your life. Ask that person to share how God has resurrected hope in his or her life. Then pray together.

87 God Protects Me

And David said, "The LORD who saved me from the paw of the lion and the paw of the bear, He will save me from the hand of this Philistine." So Saul said to David, "Go, and may the LORD be with you."

1 Samuel 17:37 NASB

When you are in the midst of a crisis or you are facing an onslaught of attacks, accusations or trials, where do you turn? Do you rely on your own strength or try to take the battle into your own hands?

In this passage, David encountered the giant Goliath. Behind the giant stood the Philistine army. For forty days, the warriors of Israel had lived under a shadow of intimidation and fear because of Goliath's daily threats, but David boldly stepped into the fight and declared that God would be his protection.

David was not speaking from a place of blind faith or drummed-up optimism. He spoke with familiarity because he knew God's character. He had spent countless hours with God while he tended his sheep. He had seen God protect and deliver him on numerous occasions. David lived in intimacy, confidence and surrender because he and God had a history together.

As you face today's giant, remember the moments when God has been your Protector. Remember these moments from your past or speak them aloud as David did, and declare God's protection in your present situation. He has not failed you before, and He will not fail you now.

▶ REFLECT

Where in my life do I need the protection of God?

▶ PRAY

Father, thank You for the countless times when You have protected me. So many times I have not even been aware of Your protection. You are a good Father. You invite me to rest in Your arms in total peace, even in the midst of storms. Thank You for shielding me and being my perfect defense.

▶ DECLARE

God protects me from the attacks of the enemy.

▶ ACT

Write down a valiant response to a giant in your life (like what David said to Saul and Goliath). Then speak it out loud as if that enemy was standing before you.

88 The God Who Remembers

Then those who feared the LORD talked with each other, and the LORD listened and heard. A scroll of remembrance was written in his presence concerning those who feared the LORD and honored his name.

Malachi 3:16 NIV

Have you ever felt forgotten? Whether you are in a season of grief or of busyness, others may forget to check in on you. Although others may forget, you can be confident that the Lord *always* remembers you.

Jesus told His disciples that every hair on their heads was numbered, illustrating how intimately He loved and valued them (see Luke 12:7). The Lord knows you, and He loves you with the same attention to detail. Among billions of people, He knows your smile, your eyes, your greatest joys and your deepest fears. He remembers you when you are grieving and when you are happy, when you are overwhelmed and when you are at rest. You never fall through the cracks.

Because this truth is so breathtaking, it may be hard to fully take hold of. The fact that God remembers you among billions is hard to comprehend through a human lens, but it is a solid truth expressed again and again in Scripture.

Ask God to give you eyes to see and a heart to understand how He remembers you so that you may fully embrace the hope that even though others may forget you, He never will.

▶ REFLECT

How has God shown me that He remembers me?

▶ PRAY

Father God, it is hard for me to comprehend the marvelous truth that You love me, know me and will never forget me. Strike me anew with the power of this truth, reminding me of times when You have worked intimately in my story, that I may face today from a place of joy and confidence in Your love.

▶ DECLARE

I am always on God's mind.

▶ ACT

Ask someone, "Has something ever happened in your life that made you feel as if God was thinking about you?" Ask him or her to tell you the story.

Hope for a Brighter Future

> Then Boaz said to the leaders and all the others there, "You are all witnesses today that I have bought from Naomi everything that belonged to Elimelech and to his sons Chilion and Mahlon. In addition, Ruth the Moabite, Mahlon's widow, becomes my wife. This will keep the property in the dead man's family, and his family line will continue among his people and in his hometown."
>
> Ruth 4:9–10 GNT

No matter what poverty, suffering or heartbreak you are facing, with God, you always have hope for the future.

Ruth and Naomi were condemned to a life of poverty after their husbands died. They were left to live out their lives as lowly field workers at best or beggars at worst.

Yet an unlikely event transformed their lives and made them part of Jesus' bloodline. Naomi's relative Boaz married Ruth and restored her and Naomi both financially and socially. This deliverance is actually a picture of the redemption that was fully realized in the life and ministry of Ruth and Boaz's descendant Jesus.

The work of Christianity, at its core, is Boaz-like, intended to restore individuals overlooked by wealth and power to a place of oneness with their Creator. This oneness has the potential to restore and propel those individuals into lives of significance that would have been unattainable without the impact of Jesus.

Just as Boaz redeemed Naomi and Ruth and secured their future, your Savior has redeemed you and has promised you an eternal future with Him.

▶ REFLECT

What examples of Boaz-like redemption have I seen in my everyday life?

▶ PRAY

Father God, I thank You for illustrating Your redemptive love through the account of Boaz and Ruth. May I continually be reminded of the great hope You have given me for the future, that one day, You will make all things new. Use me as a conduit of Your redemption for those whom I encounter today. Amen.

▶ DECLARE

With God, I always have hope for the future.

▶ ACT

Reach out to someone who is struggling financially or emotionally and provide them with something they need, whether it is a meal, a tank of gas or a listening ear.

90 God Is with Me

"Have I not commanded you? Be strong and courageous! Do not tremble or be dismayed, for the Lord your God is with you wherever you go."

Joshua 1:9 NASB

Has God ever called you to do something scary? Has He called you to speak to a stranger, confront a wrong or give beyond your means? Has His calling for your life ever felt too big?

In the first nine verses of Joshua 1, God commanded Joshua three separate times to "be strong and courageous." This was a big moment for Joshua and the people of Israel. After years of wandering in the desert, Moses was dead, and Joshua was now stepping into his God-ordained role as the leader of God's people. The time to enter their land of destiny had finally come, and the Lord repeatedly assured His children that they would not be alone.

God did not promise it would be easy. He did not promise it would be comfortable or that they would stroll into the Promised Land without struggle. He commanded His people to be courageous and not to give in to fear when things became hard.

When God's calling feels more like a burden than a blessing, remember who called you. He will not send you into the land He promised without going before you and standing beside you.

▶ REFLECT

In what areas of my life is God directing me to be strong and courageous?

▶ PRAY

Father, sometimes the things You call me to do feel scary. Help me to feel Your presence, and surround me as I take steps of obedience today. I know You are with me. You have gone before me, and You will not let me fall. Make me aware of Your closeness and protection as I move throughout my day.

▶ DECLARE

God's presence surrounds me today.

▶ ACT

Think of something God has called you to recently that stretches you beyond your capabilities or your comfort zone. Take one step toward that calling today with strength and courage.

SPECIAL INVITATION

As you read this book, you may have realized that you want to go deeper in your relationship with God, or that you have yet to welcome Jesus into your life and follow Him as King.

In the beginning, God created the world, and everything was good (see Genesis 1–2). But after the first humans disobeyed God, sin entered the world, which separated us from God and brought eternal death (see Genesis 3; Romans 3:23; 5:12; 6:23).

The good news is that "God so loved the world, that he gave his only Son [Jesus], that whoever believes in him should not perish but have eternal life" (John 3:16 ESV). Jesus came to earth, lived a sinless life and was crucified, receiving the punishment for our sins. He rose from the dead, defeating sin and death, and will return as King.

Will you receive Jesus as your Lord and Savior? Share your heart with God in this prayer: *Jesus, I no longer want to do things my way, and I choose to follow You as my Lord. Forgive me and fill me with Your Holy Spirit to live for You every day.*

To discover resources to help you grow in your faith, visit

- Bible.com or the YouVersion Bible app
- Messengerx.com or the MessengerX app
- Faithful.co or the Faithful app
- Chosenbooks.com